Gender Fairness
in Today's School

Other Books by This Author

How Political Correctness Weakens Schools: Stop Losing and Start Winning Educational Excellence (2016)
Common Sense about Common Core: Overcoming Education's Politics (2016)
Education's Flashpoints: Upside Down or Set-Up to Fail (2014)
Being Fair with Kids: The Effects of Poor Leadership in Rule Making (2013)

Gender Fairness in Today's School

A Breach of Trust for Male Students

Jim Dueck

ROWMAN & LITTLEFIELD
Lanham • Boulder • New York • London

Published by Rowman & Littlefield
A wholly owned subsidiary of The Rowman & Littlefield Publishing Group, Inc.
4501 Forbes Boulevard, Suite 200, Lanham, Maryland 20706
www.rowman.com

Unit A, Whitacre Mews, 26-34 Stannary Street, London SE11 4AB

British Library Cataloguing in Publication Information Available

Library of Congress Cataloging-in-Publication Data Available
ISBN 9781475836950 (cloth : alk. paper)
ISBN 9781475836967 (pbk. : alk. paper)
ISBN 9781475836974 (electronic)

The paper used in this publication meets the minimum requirements of American National Standard for Information Sciences—Permanence of Paper for Printed Library Materials, ANSI/NISO Z39.48-1992.

Printed in the United States of America

Contents

Preface

Forty years as an educator made me acutely aware of the plethora of issues evident in accountability within the education system. Service in the classroom, principal's office, superintendent's chair, and educational leadership for a Canadian province as an assistant deputy minister provided me with practical perspectives from all levels within the school system.

When I was a superintendent, the auditor general's office for British Columbia identified me as the "most accountable superintendent" in the province, and he arranged for a team from his office to interview stakeholders within the district. My program included providing financial incentives to schools for successfully improving student outcomes. Several suggestions for improving provincial outcomes were later implemented, including common assessments and reporting on school performance.

When I provided leadership at the provincial level, school and district "report cards" were introduced, featuring a combination of both *raw*—relative to fixed standards—and *gain*—relative to past performance—scores. This effort was one of the world's first to measure improvement and provide an evaluation of schools and school districts based on multiple levels of performance. The success of this initiative resulted in approximately fifty delegations from around the world seeking to learn from us how educational accountability can work.

These delegations included Governor Tim Pawlenty, later a candidate for the U.S. presidency, who wanted to learn about pay-for-performance in education; staff from the office of the United Kingdom's prime minister George Brown; and the minister of education from the United Kingdom, who subsequently requested me to give a personal presentation on accountability in the House of Commons for the purpose of "infecting government bureaucrats."

Later, Linda Darling-Hammond, a well-known researcher in education and a special consultant for then-President Obama's Race to the Top, requested me to give a presentation to aides in the White House, in Congress, and to the Governors Association, particularly focused on common assessment. This presentation was then followed by a request from the Department of Education for me to assist in the launch of Race to the Top, as well as to sit on the panel that identified pilots for common assessment. Out of these activities came further invitations to identify winners of the various grants associated with the Race to the Top program.

Upon my retirement, my role as a consultant allowed me the opportunity to help candidates in civic politics, to write editorials for newspapers, and to write four books. My first book—*Being Fair with Kids*—provides the research base to help parents understand that a student's birth month is an important variable in the student's success. The book concludes with a model for achieving a 60 percent reduction in student failure, a minimum 5 percent improvement in student achievement, and, consequently, a savings to a school district's budget of more than 5 percent annually.

My second book—*Education's Flashpoints*—identifies many contentious issues in education and their impact across several countries. The central problem I identified is that teachers' unions exist to represent their members, not students, and this bias prevents the school system from being highly accountable and transparent in its success in educating students. Politicians facilitate this ongoing flaw in the system because they covet teachers' votes, and so they do little to inform the general population of the data surrounding many issues that might endanger their political support.

My third book—*Common Sense about Common Core*—focuses on the contentious initiative requested by governors across the United States to have common educational standards established across participating states. While many states continue this implementation, the U.S. Congress moved to limit the federal government's involvement, which had been focused on selecting common assessment pilots and report cards for increased accountability in schools and school districts. However, after the 2016 election, there has been a degree of uncertainty concerning this emphasis on accountability, even as many states proceed with the Common Core program.

My fourth book—*How Political Correctness Weakens Schools*—identifies a myriad of issues in which political correctness interferes with decisions to improve the school systems' outcomes. Rather than focusing on the best needs of our education system's clients—students, parents, taxpayers, employers, and postsecondary programs—the government's focus has been on stakeholders—educators, teachers' unions, and special-interests groups—as these stakeholders have a vote and will likely cast their ballots based on educational matters. The media are also complicit in this misplaced perspective, because while these special interests represent a sizable viewership that generates a media company's profits, students typically do not.

These experiences of mine, coupled with a lifetime of research, provide the philosophical basis for this, my latest book. Its central message focuses on the widespread existence of grade inflation in our schools, along with the fact that this educational malady may be considerably reduced with system-wide testing. Our greatest concern with grade inflation should be that it is not equally applied to all students, but that it gives a significant advantage to female students, as they typically demonstrate more compliant behavior, for which they are rewarded. Conflating behavior with academic marks for achievement is unfair to male students, who tend to be less in tune with teachers' biases.

The lack of male teachers is another major issue presented in this book. Seldom are primary-school students the beneficiaries of instruction from male teachers who can generate an enthusiasm for learning and greater cooperation in the classroom, so that compliant behavior is less of an issue. Therefore, fairness to students also requires a greater balance in teacher gender.

Introduction

This was a difficult book to write because of centuries, indeed millennia, of female subjugation by males. Dealing with gender fairness cannot disregard the historical record of such injustice in all aspects of life, and, therefore, a decision was required to determine the extent of our world's mea culpa. An entire book and more could be devoted to a discussion of the world's unfairness to females, and the public record is replete with both past and current injustices. Therefore, it was decided to begin this book with a brief acknowledgment of this historical injustice and the posing of the question as to whether or not pursuing male injustice in the school system is now an allowable response.

The answer to this question follows with a chapter outlining how primary-school male students are disadvantaged in their learning—most notably in reading—because of the lack of opportunity for classroom instruction by male teachers. Differences in teaching styles, selection of classroom resources, and role modeling are issues addressed in this chapter.

Several chapters follow in which the degree of grade inflation is demonstrated, including in large-scale student populations in two Canadian provinces that have very high levels of student achievement in Programme for International Assessment (PISA) results. In both instances, comparison studies reveal the degree to which gender differences are evident between classroom assessments by teachers and standardized tests accompanied with anonymous marking.

In addition to these specific studies of students in Canadian provinces, another chapter is devoted to the evident wide-scale nature of grade inflation and gender discrepancy. These problems are well documented across North America and Europe, and they suggest that student marks related to academic achievement are directly tied to how compliant students are in the classroom.

The outcomes of assessing student achievement through a biased perspective are evident in a reduced number of male students qualifying for high-school courses leading to university acceptance, and fewer males participating in upper-level courses that would qualify them for awards, scholarships, and placements in prestigious universities. Finally, the ultimate outcome is a frustrated population of males who should be actively participating in the workforce but instead have opted out and are referred to as "missing men."

Providing research and documenting the problem of how our school system is failing its male students is only possible when we can compare students' classroom marks from the teacher and their marks scored on system testing with anonymous marking procedures. Identifying consistent patterns is the easy work, but recommending how the documented unfairness can be ameliorated is more difficult. The last chapter of this book provides suggested courses of action for governments with regard to education programs.

In an effort to assist readers, numerous helps have been provided throughout the book. With the exception of the brief chapter 9, readers will benefit from reviewing an end-of-chapter list of the critical points discussed in each chapter. Longer chapters also include subheadings to aid readers in identifying the main ideas. Further, italicizing key words and phrases is another technique used extensively to assist readers in capturing key ideas.

The citation of external resources follows a relatively consistent pattern throughout the book. Summarizing critical points made by external references is one means of providing others' perspectives; however, in most instances, the actual words of the reference are quoted. Finally, while few researchers have traced this unfairness-to-males issue from childhood to adulthood, a lengthy listing of references is included at the end of the book to provide a list of those researchers who are concerned with some aspect of the issue. With much of the book's content derived from the author's data analysis conducted in large student populations, an extensive listing of other researchers expressing similar perspectives is noteworthy.

Chapter 1

Gender Issues Are Sensitive

Featuring gender-related academic differences and advantages poses risks, because people frequently adopt defensive positions, labeling a book as sexist and coming up with excuses to disregard current research on the subject. Readers with such tendencies will find opportunity to dismiss this book's findings, because the presentation of data demonstrates a shortcoming in our school system that disadvantages male students as early as their first year in school and well into their final term, when they are competing with other students for college and career opportunities.

The intention of this chapter is to reveal how teaching practices in a female-dominated environment impede male students in achieving their educational potential. A second key issue demonstrates how male students' lack of compliant behavior prevents many males from securing financing for college and entry to higher-level careers. These findings regarding unfairness suggest that it is not intentional, because educators are motivated to help all students succeed; rather, these issues can only be exposed through systematic standardized testing processes that require careful analysis of this type of assessment, which most educators wish to avoid.

Assessing student learning, while highly contentious within the education system, is not a well-understood activity in the public arena. Consternation exists within the school system about divulging details of how students' work is evaluated. However, inconsistent practices and unreliable assessments by educators are clearly articulated in the literature, and this is a central theme of this book. Poor and unfair practices in our classrooms continue, because *students, parents, and the public are generally kept unaware of the subtle implications of students' work being assessed inconsistently.*

The emotionally charged nature of this issue—assessing students' work fairly and consistently—was especially evident during a personal conversation

1

I had with a teachers' union representative, who expressed displeasure with releasing statistical information that had been distributed at a meeting of education stakeholders. His perceived outcome of seeing actual data discussed in an open forum was that their public release would result in a "loss of confidence in the school system." Reform is hindered when such protectionist thinking permeates our schools, and, in this case, it perpetuates unfairness toward many students.

Trust should be on a slippery slope whenever public-sector workers conspire to *lessen transparency*. Public education contains voluminous information from which conclusions regarding quality of service can be ascertained, yet seldom does the education system undertake self-analysis where *unwelcome findings are simplistically portrayed* in the public arena. Too frequently, the media are complicit in keeping educational statistics from public scrutiny, because educators comprise a significant portion of the workforce—approximately 3 percent—and thus are a significant part of the media's revenue-generating subscribers.

An analysis of assessment information can demonstrate how students are affected, which, in this book, demonstrates that there are definite winners and losers in the educational system. Students seldom pay the subscriptions, and editors are hesitant about rocking the educators' collective boat by publishing controversial news regarding their incompetence. It does not make sense—or "cents"—for the media to release controversial information, when loyalty from such a large subscriber group may be threatened. A discussion of this sensitive issue with one media mogul revealed his response: "We know who our readers are, and we will not print letters [to the editor] which will offend them."

Full disclosure within education is also hampered by its employers—i.e., politicians at the school district or provincial/state levels. Their primary motivation is to have their organization function as a well-oiled machine, without glitches that might draw public attention. *No news is usually good news at reelection time*, and any visible attempt to cover up the unfair treatment of students could produce sufficient backlash to unseat incumbents. Despite their public pronouncements regarding their unqualified commitment to students, important information concerning the quality of educational services, which could be open to a negative spin, is frequently left unreported.

Nevertheless, hidden within the databases of many educational systems is the quantifiable evidence that *student achievement is assessed inconsistently and with bias*. Attempts to unearth this data encounter many obstacles when bureaucrats discover how these requests could produce embarrassment and calls for reform. While there are many issues within school systems about which the data demonstrate poor management, none is more unsettling than the lack of fairness perpetrated against students while engaged in their learning.

Specifically, an overwhelming disproportionate representation in the teaching of the two genders, *especially in the early grades*, is an important issue addressed by this book. A predominantly female workforce in the field of education provides few role models for male students, and it utilizes teaching strategies and responses to classroom behaviors more aligned with female students—to the detriment of male students.

A second focus of this book concerns the prevalence of *low standards* of learning in classrooms where ample evidence suggests that marks are consistently inflated; however, *this inflation is not applied equally across subgroups of students*. Evidence demonstrates bias related to behavior that, in turn, documents a gender advantage, creating implications that yield lifelong consequences, not only to individuals but also to our society as a whole.

Equally important to societal conditions is our tacit acceptance that gender bias is appropriate and a fact of life, as this leads to scant opportunities for change. In fact, any pronounced effort at reforming the current bias could produce a corresponding backlash, based upon a history of prejudice, to a time when gender equality did not exist, and such efforts now could be viewed as "what was fair for the goose is now, indeed, fair for the gander." Emotions regarding this historical unfairness run deep, and they serve well for those who see "payback" as a logical outcome. It is here that our story regarding educational bias must begin.

THE KEY POINTS MADE IN THIS CHAPTER ARE:

- Males experience some unfair predicaments in our present-day school system.
- Data demonstrating the unfair nature of these predicaments are usually left unreported, to avoid public controversy and a loss of confidence in the school system.
- Concerns about fairness are typically unreported, because educators comprise a significant percentage of not only voters but also subscribers to print and visual media.
- Basic issues producing unfairness to male students are connected to the disproportionate representation of females in the workplace and teachers' responses to student behaviors.

Chapter 2

Two Wrongs Don't Equal a Right

Gender inequity outlining disadvantages experienced by females in our culture warrants an entire book, because there can be no denying its long-standing existence. Recognizable inequalities evident in the right to vote, participation in management jobs, equality in pay, enrollment in colleges and universities, and the holding of public office are just some examples of how females endured unfairness in our society. However, these examples, as significant as they may be, pale in comparison with what has occurred in the legal system regarding spousal abuse, sexual harassment, and rape.

Some cultures around the world have yet to even dent their ceilings of unfairness, and females experience a lower status to the extreme. Forced full-body coverings, walking a certain distance behind male companions, and the denial of equal access to education are examples of how far behind some cultures still are; they have a long way to go before they can even gain ground in the issues still haunting civilized cultures.

The point of this brief chapter is first *to acknowledge millennia of unfair gender conditions* that are gradually being ameliorated through government action and, sometimes, through common sense. Much remains to be done, however, and there are constant reminders of remaining inequities whenever elections are held.

The school system is *a vehicle for societal change, and it has accomplished much for the female gender* at both the student and employee levels. At the turn of this past century, when it was noted that female students lacked proportional representation in technology, mathematics, and some sciences, special efforts toward enrolling female students in these programs have been making progress to achieve greater gender balance. Initially, females' interest in these subject areas centered on work in medicine; however, considerable diversification into more typically male-dominated areas—including engineering, business, etc.—is now increasing.

Now, however, the issue is whether the unfairness that prevailed throughout the ages should cause us to disregard a situation that has become unfair to male students. Is "continued payback" an appropriate mentality in this area? If our school systems can be shown to condone an unfair learning advantage skewed toward females, in which male students are perennially victimized, should processes be incorporated for leveling the playing field of opportunities? Experience with several governments concerning the focus of this book has already indicated their desire to ignore using their own data as sufficient grounds for blazing a trail in righting the wrongs being perpetuated against male students. In other words, most politicians *avoid publicly referencing gender issues that suggest a disadvantage to male students.*

Findings revealed in this book are only possible because of the concerted effort toward *increasing accountability* in education and literally *badgering* for information not generally released to the public. Their bearing on our society, discussed in chapter 8, is already evident in disturbingly negative outcomes that threaten a well-functioning society. Ignoring the threat toward our current students' generation will unsettle our values and mores for decades to come.

This chapter *is intentionally brief because there is no disagreement* that the female gender has experienced millennia of unfair treatment, and any effort to describe this inequity would require a book on its own. It is what it is. The lesson, however, is that *we must remain vigilant* in identifying *all unfairness* regarding gender issues and resolve them when they occur. This book is focused on an unfair predicament involving male students at a time when political correctness is more inclined to discuss only those issues in which females are treated unfairly.

THE KEY POINTS MADE IN THIS CHAPTER ARE:

- Gender inequity outlining disadvantages experienced by females in our culture is a long-standing issue.
- The school system is a vehicle for societal change, and it has accomplished much for the female gender at both the student and employee levels.
- A successful effort has been launched to achieve female parity in the sciences, mathematics, and technology.
- Now, however, the issue is whether or not the unfairness toward males currently evident in the school system should be disregarded.

Chapter 3

Teacher Gender and Fairness to Boys

This chapter unveils a concern frequently discussed within the school system; yet it persists because decades of practice have passed without adequate research to ascertain the impact on students' learning outcomes. Specifically, does gender impact fairness? In other words, is student success related to the gender of the teacher or the student? Do the data demonstrate trends that place one gender *at risk for fairness*? Are some students disadvantaged in their learning because of their teacher's gender?

A 2007 national StatCan report titled "Why Are Most University Students Women?" disclosed similar findings to a regional study that found females achieving significantly higher levels in *reading* on standardized tests for all three grade levels (3/6/9). The matter of poorer performance by males on standardized reading tests requires an explanation, because it is gender-related. The StatCan report postulates reasons for this disadvantage:

> The relative challenges that boys face early in life may be exacerbated during the elementary school years for at least two reasons. First, 83% of elementary school teachers are women (2001 Census). This means that girls are far more likely to be taught by a same-sex teacher than boys during the first several years of school.... A recent U.S. study using the National Education Longitudinal Survey found that both boys and girls benefited from a same-sex teacher (Dee 2005). The size of the effect was quite large. For example, it is estimated that just one year with a male English teacher would eliminate nearly one-third of the gender gap in reading performance among 13-year-olds and would do so by improving the performance of boys and simultaneously harming that of girls.... Second, independent of the teacher's gender, the natural assets of girls may be better suited for mainstream teaching strategies. In contrast, the natural assets of boys may be treated as problems in the school system. According to Julien and Ertl (2000), 10 to 11-year-old boys are less likely to work neatly and carefully

(61%) than girls (82%), are more likely to get into many fights (35%) than girls (13%), are more likely to be restless, unable to sit still or display hyperactivity (49%) than girls (23%), and are less likely to show sympathy when someone else has made a mistake (32%) than girls (49%).... Findings in the current study suggest that a very large proportion of the gender gap in university participation relates to non-cognitive abilities displayed at school. As a result, understanding the female advantage in attending university may critically depend on understanding why girls outperform boys in elementary and high school. (Frenette and Zeman 2007)

This national study introduces a thesis concerned with explaining the gender gap in postsecondary institutions. It proposes that the issues outlined in this book relate to noncognitive abilities and behaviors displayed by students while in the school system. In other words, it suggests, teachers are *conflating achievement and behavior* that gives a distinct disadvantage to male students. Is this a fair practice?

This StatCan report supports regional findings that conclude there is a definitive *female advantage, from school-generated marks based on compliant behaviors.* Early in their careers as students, boys are disadvantaged when their learning is assessed because teachers allow, perhaps unwittingly, students' less compliant behaviors to be *conflated* with assessments of achievement. An important message in this book is that allowing behavior to influence assessments of learning is unfair, and reforms must be incorporated to overcome this unacceptable situation, because it influences self-esteem and attitudes about future learning in male students.

This Canadian report also reminds us that male students are disadvantaged by having fewer occasions to receive reading instruction from male teachers, especially in the early elementary grades. This fact is powerful evidence of how the Canadian school system *narrows career opportunities for its male students—yet it is incapable of changing what is clearly an unfair learning condition for a significant portion of its students.* The situation in the United States is similar.

Specificity regarding this disadvantage in reading is presented by Johnson (2009), who provides this report on studies about what children read:

> Girls most often choose novels, while boys prefer a broader range of genres that includes sports, hobbies, and craft books, as well as cartoons and newsy things. But that's a problem ... because teachers and librarians rarely deem these books worthy of study in school. It's not clear why a novel is more appropriate reading material for the classroom than non-fiction would be, but it's certainly assumed that it is.

King and Gurian (2006) examined teaching *strategies* and discovered that classrooms were generally a better fit for the verbal-emotive, sit-still, take-notes, listen-carefully, multitasking girl. Teachers tended to view the natural assets that boys bring to the learning—impulsivity, single-task focus, spatial-kinesthetic learning, and physical aggression—as problems.

By altering strategies to accommodate these typically male assets, *the gender gap was successfully closed in just one year.* Their strategy capitalized on boys' "R-rated minds," referring to a preference for "aggression scenarios, competition, action, and superhero journeys."

The Canadian Council on Learning also examined gender differences in reading achievement and reported how classrooms vary with their reading material:

A recent study in the United States found that the genres preferred by boys were available in only one-third of classrooms in part because teachers and librarians disapprove of them as appropriate forms of school-based reading. Others have claimed that these genres do not usually find their way into classrooms or library shelves because teachers are predominantly female and teachers' own reading preferences are reflected in the books they select for their students. (*Lessons* 2009)

Availability of appropriate reading materials has the capacity to reduce the disadvantage that boys experience in reading success, and reducing the significant imbalance in teacher gender can provide yet another strategy. Children attach themselves to role models, and when *boys see male teachers* interested in reading, they "catch" the importance of reading. Many schools understand this and attempt to compensate by bringing male athletes and other prominent men into the classroom to read to the students. For example, any recollections of the infamous day of 9/11 will always show U.S. president George W. Bush being told of the terrorist actions *while reading to kindergarten students.*

Teacher hiring practices in North America follow a free-market principle: People who want to pursue a career in education register for training programs, graduate, and then enter the market, seeking employment in the schools where they hope to be hired. Prospective employers examine credentials and attempt to match the applicants with their needs. Gender may be one of these "needs," but the current prevailing culture discourages specifying it. In the United States, the National Center for Education Information reported in 2005 that 82 percent of public school teachers were female. This percentage was up from 69 percent in 1986 and 74 percent in 1996. In Canada, almost three-quarters of teachers are currently female.

Working with young children is generally considered to be a female role; it is not surprising, then, that there are more females teaching in our elementary schools. An important question pertains to the appropriate ratio, however. At what point is there an imbalance that does a disservice to a large portion of the student population? In education, are male students disadvantaged by the lack of male teachers? Simply, is conventional thought—that raising children, including the provision of their education, is most appropriately handled by females—still applicable?

Children's earliest years in school are critical for their future success. During their primary-school career, they not only develop foundational knowledge and skills for academic success, but they also develop an understanding of how to relate to and behave with others. Who their role models are is an important aspect in the process of becoming confident, competent, and contributing members of our communities.

It is in these earliest years that our concern is more acute. A study by Thomas Dee (Feller 2006) showed that preschool- and elementary-aged schoolchildren are taught by females in almost 80 percent of the classrooms. In the United Kingdom, Cassidy (2008) reported that 84 percent of primary teachers were women. In Australia, Porter (2015) indicates that fewer than one in five of 2014's primary teachers in Victoria were male. A critical question is whether male students are systematically disadvantaged by not engaging with male teachers during these critical years in their primary education.

TEACHER GENDER AND STUDENT LEARNING

Before answering this question, Hoffmann and Oreopoulos (2009) provide insight into whether the instructor's gender has any impact on outcomes between males and females at the university level. If there is a relationship within this age group, where students are more advanced in their academic abilities, it would serve to magnify the impact with very young children. Older students have more sophisticated coping mechanisms than are evident in younger children, and we could expect that the gender issue would be more neutralized.

These researchers addressed the importance of gender interactions between teachers and students at the *college level* to explain educational performance and subject interest. They found that

> assignment to a same-sex instructor boosts relative grade performance and the likelihood of completing a course, but the magnitudes of these effects are small. A same-sex instructor increases average grade performance by at most 5 percent of its standard deviation and decreases the likelihood of dropping a course by 1.2 percentage points.

There is some positive effect when students have a same-sex instructor, but it is not significant in this older age group, which is both more mature and considerably less varied in academic performance. Whereas more elite students enter postsecondary education, the school system serves all students with their *entire range of student abilities*. Not only does the school system educate the weak students, but this research likely dealt with only one year rather than the multiple *consecutive years* in which males are in elementary school with female teachers.

These authors proceeded to compare their results with Thomas Dee, who studied this gender issue in primary-school children. Hoffmann and Oreopoulos (2009) state:

> Our grade score estimates are somewhat smaller than the 5 to 10 percent standard deviation effects reported by Dee (2007) at the primary school level (using similar methodology), but not by much. Two possibilities may explain the difference. First, same-sex instructors may matter more at earlier ages, when development of cognitive and non-cognitive ability occurs more rapidly. Second, reactions from students over the gender of a teacher may matter less than reactions from teachers over the gender of a student. As mentioned earlier, college instructors do not typically interact on a one-on-one basis with students in large first year classes and do not typically grade tests, so there is less chance of discrimination. Another result that matches some of Dee's findings is that the interaction effect seems to stem more from male students performing worse with female instructors, while female performance appears unaffected.

Because approximately only one in ten elementary-school teachers is male, it is likely true that the imbalance is considerably lower in *grade 1*; yet this is an important year for children. When their success is curtailed by not benefiting from a same-gender teacher at this earliest stage in their school career, there is little likelihood of receiving a compensatory boost from working with a male teacher in grades 2 and beyond.

This gender issue was also reviewed by the 2007 StatCan report—"Why Are Most University Students Women?"—which also referenced another report by Dee and indicated further that

> a recent U.S. study using the National Education Longitudinal Survey found that both boys and girls benefited from a same-sex teacher (Dee 2005). The size of the effect was quite large. For example, it is estimated that just one year with a male English teacher would eliminate nearly one-third of the gender gap in reading performance among 13-year-olds and would do so by improving the performance of boys and simultaneously harming that of girls. Similarly, a year with a female teacher would help girls partially catch up to boys in science and mathematics. Specifically, it would close the gender gap in science achievement

among 13-year-olds by one half and entirely eliminate the smaller achievement gap in mathematics.

Dee went on to state,

> Indeed, my results confirm that a teacher's gender does have large effects on student test performance, teacher perceptions of students, and students' engagement with academic material. Simply put, girls have better educational outcomes when taught by women and boys are better off when taught by men.

There is no equivocating in Dee's findings that student success is related to teachers' gender.

In the United Kingdom, this gender issue was studied from another perspective, in which the focus was aimed at discovering how youngsters' effort, motivation, and educational achievements were shaped. This study, reported in the *Daily Mail* on November 13, 2010, concluded that when working with male teachers, the following applies:

> Children had a more "positive perception of the rewards" of their effort despite the fact the males were not any more lenient. Both boys and girls also showed greater confidence in their ability. Researchers said the findings were "new and significant" as the effects were evident for every male teacher in the experiment. They said the study "reveals that pupils taught by male teachers tend to have better perceptions of the importance of hard work, better perceptions of equalities of opportunities and higher self-esteem. This experiment shows that male teachers may be beneficial for both male and female pupils, increasing motivation and effort." ("Pupils" 2010)

The same newspaper article referenced an American study at Kent University, which reported:

> Women teachers are holding back boys by reprimanding them for typically male behaviour. They are reinforcing stereotypes that boys are "silly" in class and refuse to "sit nicely like the girls" and are more likely to indulge in pranks. Researchers found that women teachers may also unwittingly perpetuate low expectations of boys and encourage girls to work harder by telling them they are clever.

Lawson (2013) summarizes a PISA international study reinforcing the theme that girls get higher marks than boys *because they are better behaved*. The Organisation for Economic Co-operation and Development (OECD), which carried out the research, stated that the bias could have "far-reaching effects" for boys' self-esteem. It could also cause them to miss out on university places or change their career ambitions, as lower marks may cause students to lower their aims accordingly.

The OECD report highlighted the fact that

perhaps the most crucial finding of the report is that socio-economically advantaged students and girls are more likely to receive better marks from their teachers, even when compared to socio-economically disadvantaged students or boys who perform equally well in PISA and report similar attitudes and behaviours. What this suggests is that teachers give higher-than-expected marks to girls and socio-economically advantaged students, possibly because they tend to reward, on top of performance and the set of attitudes and behaviours that are measured by PISA, other attitudes and behaviours that girls and advantaged students are most likely to adopt. Whatever the reason, inequalities in marking practices may lead to inequalities in educational expectations, and, later, to inequalities in educational attainment and labour-market outcomes, thus perpetuating social disparities and reducing opportunities for upward mobility, especially among disadvantaged boys.

This PISA study analyzed countries that use many tests *set by teachers* or assessments based on *student coursework*. In Britain, for example, nearly two-thirds of girls achieve five good GCSEs, while only half of boys do so. With this information, the UK coalition government plans to *assess GCSEs almost entirely through end-of-year exams instead of including coursework marked by teachers*. Grade inflation is an educational problem exacerbated by advantaging a gender—in this case, the females, which will be revealed to a greater degree in chapter 5.

The point of this chapter is that teacher gender is an important issue in the academic success of female students. Reading is a dominant element of the elementary-school curriculum, and the selection of curriculum resources by a predominantly female teacher workforce is an identified concern. The type of resources available for reading instruction has been impacted by the advent of technology in classrooms where students now read from computer screens. Even student assessments now use technology, and approximately one half of students took the OECD tests using computers.

PISA assessments are written every three years by samples of students, from many countries around the world, when they reach fifteen years of age. A female advantage in reading is a consistent finding; however, the PISA 2015 report notes a significant change in gender results for reading. Specifically:

Between PISA 2009 and PISA 2015, the gender gap in reading narrowed by 12 points on average across OECD countries.... Among all PISA participants, a significant gap in reading performance was observed in 32 countries and economies, while there was no change in the gender gap in the remaining 29 countries and economies. (Lawson 2013)

A possible reason for this improvement in male reading ability is not projected within the report; however, the improvement does coincide with a major change in resources during the first fifteen years of this century. Use of technology in schools increased dramatically around the world, and providing students with the opportunity to utilize this medium rather than reading the words printed in traditional books may be more aligned with the interests of male students.

MALE TEACHERS FACE A GENDER MINEFIELD

The secretary of state for education in the United Kingdom, Michael Gove, responded to reports about gender bias by stating that more male teachers were needed, but specific remedies were put off by worries that teacher-pupil contact was a "legal minefield," because bathroom and clothing issues were more related to a female role. In a speech, he went on to say, "More male teachers were needed, especially in primary schools to provide children who often *lack male role models at home* with male authority figures who can display both strength and sensitivity."

This legal minefield was addressed in Canada by the editorial board of the *National Post* on February 20, 2013:

> A 2010 study by professors at Nipissing, published in the *McGill Journal of Education*, found 13% (albeit of a small sample) of teachers had faced down false accusations of inappropriate contact with their students. "For male teachers, false accusations were a reality many had come to accept as a hazard of the profession, often accompanied by a sense of constant worry that infringed on their ability and willingness to respond as they naturally might to situations that present themselves every day in their classrooms," the authors wrote. "This weariness restricted the male teacher's ability to act in ways that they otherwise more naturally might; ways in which their female colleagues were free to act without suspicion." (National Post 2013)

The editorial concluded that this *stigma will increase as the percentage of male teachers decreases.* Given that the pool of male teachers in Canadian universities is actually shrinking, the editorial board concluded that employers and unions should be "making the education system more friendly to male students and male teachers alike."

The impact of gender with younger students is a significant issue, and this book will demonstrate the path of problems emerging from the unfair educational environment facing male students. Does this concern then qualify for special action? In other words, is this a societal issue, in which factors such as salary and working conditions mitigate male involvement? Or is this a system issue, in which the educational community can alter circumstances and thus change the current imbalance? These questions likely stir up memories of a time when teachers were actually paid differently based on their gender. Overcoming this memory remains a significant hill to climb.

GENDER INEQUITIES AND DISCRIMINATION

Confounding this discussion is how the school system responded when student gender balance was examined in mathematics and science. When data emerged that male participation was significantly higher than that of females in these courses, *the feminist movement focused on the imbalance as exhibiting a form of discrimination.* The educational system responded to the criticism, either because of negative pressure or due to a legitimate concern, by doing everything possible to increase female participation in these subjects.

Tactics to level the playing field in math and science have even included establishing all-girl classes and schools. Bronson (2012), referencing studies by the National Educators' Association, reports:

> Only a dozen or so public schools in the United States had single-gender classrooms in 2002. A decade later, more than 500 public schools offered single-gender opportunities.... Girls who learn in all-girl environments are believed to be more comfortable responding to questions and sharing their opinions in class and more likely to explore more "non-traditional" subjects such as math, science, and technology. Additionally, studies suggest that boys in single-gender classrooms are more successful in school and more likely to pursue a wide range of interests and activities.... Boys tend to be less competitive and more cooperative and collaborative.

The significant imbalance in male achievement in the language arts is not a disadvantage that has just recently crept into our level of consciousness. We have known about it for decades, even before standardized testing confirmed it. One principal related his efforts to help his primary-school males be more successful in reading and writing by searching for qualified and competent male teachers. There were so few candidates available that a comprehensive search was required and, once such a male educator was identified, the principal indicated that everything possible was done to retain his services.

What was possible, however, was relatively insignificant. In fact, it was mostly relational, as the principal worked to make this teacher feel valued through positive recognition, opportunities to attend conferences, providing leadership roles within the school, etc. While undertaking these kinds of activities with all staff members makes sense, this principal believed it was necessary to go beyond the norm in order to overcome the short supply of male teachers in his elementary school.

Male students' lack of success relative to the level of success enjoyed by female students, especially in the core curricular area of reading, is a critical point of this chapter. This differential in success appears to be related to the gender of the teacher, which in early grades is almost exclusively female. Unfortunately, this differential in success also appears to be influenced by teachers' marks on student academic success conflated with student behavior.

THE KEY POINTS MADE IN THIS CHAPTER ARE:

• Our schools are predominantly staffed by female teachers, and this predominance is increasing.
• In the early grades, a teacher's gender has a large effect on student test performance, on teacher perceptions of students, and on students' engagement with academic material.
• Girls have better educational outcomes when taught by women, and boys are better off when taught by men.
• In our culture, male teachers face a "legal minefield" when working with young children.
• An imbalance favoring male students in mathematics and science has not translated into concerns regarding lower levels of achievement by males in reading.
• Females demonstrate higher levels of compliant behavior and retain a significant advantage over their male counterparts, whose behavior is conflated with academic achievement.

Chapter 4

Blind Spot

Classroom proficiency in assessing student learning is an issue facing educators today that is creating significant anxiety within their profession. Can we unconditionally *trust* a teacher's judgment when assessing students' learning to the degree that it is warranted? Accountability in education is a new reality, and instituting programs that inspect an educator's expertise creates a degree of insecurity. *What takes place in classrooms is no longer as private as it once was.* There is a greater emphasis on transparency, and placing certain aspects of teaching under a microscope produces a subtle but noticeable impact on teachers' working conditions.

The purpose of this chapter is to answer a significant question concerning the expertise that teachers bring to their responsibility of assessing students' work fairly. Are the standards used when marking students' work too high or too low? In other words, are the grades given to students inflated or deflated, thereby causing inconsistencies throughout the school system and providing some students with a distinct advantage? Marks are a student's currency, and consistency in earning these marks is the mandate that must be expected of our school system.

THE TALE OF TWO CANADIAN PROVINCES

This chapter's focus is on two western Canadian provinces whose students are high-level achievers on the OECD's international PISA tests for fifteen-year-old students in reading, mathematics, and science. British Columbia and Alberta have each participated in these tests since their inception in the 1990s, but the provinces' success in PISA 2015 is the focus of this chapter. Canada is the only country in the advanced world that does not have a federal office of education; therefore, each province oversamples its student population so that results qualify to be compared with all other nations. OECD describes these provinces as "economic regions."

British Columbia is Canada's coastal province, with approximately 616,000 full-time students having been enrolled in the 2016–2017 school system, whereas approximately 676,000 attended the Alberta school system. The student population in these two provinces would place them at the midpoint of the populace of states in the United States and similar in enrollment to Utah. The size of the student populations in these two provinces provides a valid study regarding what happens when assessing the academic progress of students.

When examining academic success using PISA 2015 *science*, students in these two provinces tested at an *elite level*, with Alberta placing second and British Columbia third behind Singapore. In *reading*, British Columbia topped the world, just marginally ahead of Singapore, which was just marginally ahead of third-place Alberta. In *mathematics*, British Columbia ranked ninth in the world, and slightly ahead of Alberta, which was fourteenth. These high levels of achievement are typical for the seven occasions when PISA was administered, beginning in 1997, and now include seventy-eight countries, and they merely provide some context, demonstrating that students in these two provinces consistently benefit from excellent school systems.

Both provinces employ a form of standardized testing during grades 3 through 9, as well as do senior high-school students; this is a feature not evident in most provinces across the country. These tests provide opportunities to quantify *differences between marks earned on the system tests, and classroom marks awarded by teachers.* Patterns assist us in making inferences about the assessment program evident in classrooms, and they provide quantifiable evidence regarding the accuracy of standards employed by classroom teachers when assessing their students' learning.

ALBERTA'S CLASSROOM STANDARDS

In Alberta, diploma examinations are standardized tests utilized for two streams in grade-12 courses leading to a graduation diploma. Upper-stream courses are generally necessary for application-to-university programs. Preparation of these tests includes item development by classroom teachers, with items then subjected to rigorous field testing, and importantly, examinations are *marked anonymously* by at least *two teachers.* The superior quality of these tests was acclaimed by representatives of the U.S. Congress in 1993 and again by the U.S. Department of Education in 2009.

Contrast the quality control exercised by an examination manager whose duties are completely devoted to developing a single test, with what occurs in classrooms across provinces, states, and nations. These classroom assessments are not standardized or field-tested, and they are usually marked by *only one person who is also very familiar with the student*. The point is that quality control for validity and reliability in classroom assessments varies greatly from classroom to classroom, as well as within the provincial assessment program.

The critical question in this discussion is whether one of these two assessment approaches consistently yields higher ratings of student achievement. Judgments related to the veracity of testing approaches are possible when consistent patterns in the data emerge. During the 2015–2016 testing period, which included administrations in January concluding the first semester, and in June for semester two, an analysis for students at the Standard of Excellence (approximately an "A" rating) and at the Acceptable Standard (approximately a pass rating) provides a powerful set of conclusions.

Subjects in the upper-stream courses at the Standard of Excellence always had higher scores from the classroom teachers than were earned on system tests. The percentages of students achieving at the Standard of Excellence were *more frequently awarded from classroom teachers* as follows:

- Biology: 45 percent more from classroom teachers
- Chemistry: 44 percent more from classroom teachers
- English Language Arts: 201 percent more from classroom teachers
- Mathematics: 96 percent more from classroom teachers
- Physics: 36 percent more from classroom teachers
- Social Studies: 186 percent more from classroom teachers
- Average: 101 percent more from classroom teachers

Clearly, an arms race of A grades is taking place in classrooms. English Language Arts is a required course for university entrance, and while 10.7 percent of students earned an A on the diploma examination, classroom teachers gave almost one-third (32.2 percent) of students an A grade—more than three times as many, or 201 percent.

These alarming results for just one year (2016) provided an impetus to review patterns for the previous five school years (2011 to 2015). Figure 4.1 provides the averages during this five-year period for each upper-stream course, and demonstrates how much higher were classroom marks than provincial examination marks for both the Standard of Excellence and the Acceptable Standard. *A defensible conclusion from the analysis indicates that lower standards or expectations in classrooms and personal knowledge of the student are barriers to fair assessment.*

Diploma Subject	School Excellence above Diploma	School Acceptable above Diploma
Language Arts 30-1	181%	13%
Math 30-1	48%	24%
Social Studies 30-1	141%	16%
Biology 30	39%	23%
Chemistry 30	40%	22%
Physics 30	50%	19%

Figure 4.1   Alberta: School versus Diploma Five-Year Average (2011–2015)

For subjects in the *lower-stream courses*, which are necessary for high-school graduation but not for university applications, the percentage of students achieving at the Standard of Excellence in 2016 *were more frequently awarded from classroom teachers* as follows:

- English Language Arts: 8 percent
- Mathematics: 49 percent
- Science: 29 percent
- Social Studies: 26 percent
- Average: 28 percent

While some countries in the world use the exit-examination marks as the students' final mark, Alberta's model prior to 2015 was to use a breakdown of a 50 percent class mark and a 50 percent diploma. Political pandering for teachers' union support in the 2015 provincial election produced a change from this 50/50 split to a 70/30 one, with the classroom mark valued at 70 percent. The increased value of 2016 class marks over those awarded in classrooms in 2015 for upper-stream courses increased the variance between classroom marks and diploma examination marks. In other words, classroom works were *further inflated* for the Standard of Excellence as follows:

- Biology: 12 percent
- Chemistry: 6 percent
- English Language Arts: 5 percent
- Mathematics: 4 percent
- Physics: 5 percent
- Social Studies: 4 percent

In *one year*, following a politically motivated decision to deflate the value of provincial assessments, which undergo rigorous processes ensuring their validity and reliability, the gap between marks in *upper-stream courses*— necessary for university applications—in provincial and classroom assessments *increased an average of 6 percent*. This increase is in addition to the already significant differences recorded earlier. *The race for As is increasing!*

Janet French, with the *Edmonton Journal*, investigated this issue in an article published on February 27, 2017, titled "Are Teachers Inflating Grades?" She reported specific-level school results within the Edmonton school district:

- At Eastglen, 96 percent of students in Chemistry 30 got a passing grade in the class. Just 47 percent, however, passed the diploma exam. Everyone enrolled in Science 30 had a passing grade in the class, but less than half of the students passed the diploma exam. While 88 percent of the students in Math 30-2 had an honors-level grade in the class, just 12 percent of them achieved these honors on the diploma exam.
- Nearly half of the students enrolled in French immersion at Harry Ainlay High School had an honors grade in French Language Arts 30-1 class, yet only 4.3 percent of the students achieved an honors grade on the diploma exam.
- Before the diploma exam, it appeared that J. Percy Page students were strong in math—91 percent of Math 30-1 students passed the class, and 45 percent had achieved an honors level. More than half of those students—54 percent—however, failed the diploma exam.
- At the end of the course, 99.5 percent of Queen Elizabeth students enrolled in English 30-1 were passing. Forty percent of the students failed the diploma exam. Ninety-five percent of Math 30-1 students passed the Math 30-1 class, but more than one-third of them failed the diploma exam.
- Of Ross Sheppard students enrolled in English 30-1, 43 percent had honors-level grade in class, but only 10 percent achieved a honors level on the diploma exam. Sixty percent of French immersion students had honors in French Language Arts class, but only 8 percent had achieved an honors level on the exam.
- At Victoria School, 99 percent of the students were passing Math 30-1, and more than half of the students in the class had honors, but almost half of the students failed the diploma exam.

Readers should be reminded that Alberta's education system has a long-standing history of lower levels of grade inflation than all other Canadian jurisdictions, yet this pernicious problem is still evident in its schools.

One disappointing aspect of this increase in grade inflation is the government's response to the public's concerns about it. Stated in a letter from the deputy minister of education to this author was the commitment to help *ensure* that consistent standards for assessment are applied at the school level, Education [Department] has developed various documents that explain the standards for each diploma exam course. Education will continue to offer assessment sessions to teachers through the Alberta Regional Professional Development Consortia. Education has also initiated an Assessment Capacity Project, which is intended to further support teachers in their classroom assessment practices.

Yes, the bureaucracy was already concerned with levels of grade inflation and was initiating several countermeasures to control it, to *"ensure* that consistent standards for assessment are applied at the school level." Data comparing classroom assessments with diploma examinations for the subsequent school year clearly demonstrate that *failure to ensure consistent standards* for assessment was the unfortunate outcome of these efforts!

This factual account shows that teachers *generously* award marks equivalent to an A, which demonstrates that *classroom standards are low.* There is a logical tendency for teachers to want their students to experience success in qualifying for postsecondary learning. These results then make teachers look good on the reviews of their teaching performance.

However, at the other end of the achievement spectrum, the *failing rate* for the Acceptable Standard—the pass mark—for *upper-stream* courses averaged only 2.6 percent for the class mark, but it was almost six times greater, at 17.5 percent, on the diploma examination. For the *lower-stream* courses, the failing rate in the classroom was 4.3 percent, but the failing rate for the diploma examinations was four times greater, at 17.5 percent.

Teachers' familiarity with students is a destructive force in maintaining high standards. Marks may be a student's currency, but they are also a teacher's currency for maintaining a productive relationship with students as well as for acquiring support from parents. Unfortunately, inflated marks produce lower levels of learning, because they give students the false belief that they are doing well. More important is the answer to a question about whether grade inflation is spread equally across all students. This issue will be addressed later on.

BRITISH COLUMBIA'S CLASSROOM STANDARDS

British Columbia's examination program has utilized a hybrid approach over several years, with some provincial tests occurring during grades 10, 11, and 12. The provincial examinations in 2015 were analyzed to determine whether grade inflation in classrooms was evident by determining the percentage of students with a failing mark, which occurred more frequently with the examination than was rated by teachers' assessment in classrooms.

- English 10: Failure rate on the exam was *175 percent greater* than on the class mark.
- Math 10 (Precalculus): Failure rate on the exam was *200 percent greater* than on the class mark.
- Math 10 (Applied): Failure rate on the exam was *275 percent greater* than on the class mark.
- Science 10: Failure rate on the exam was *60 percent greater* than on the class mark.
- Social Studies 11: Failure rate on the exam was *67 percent greater* than on the class mark.
- Civic Studies 11: Failure rate on the exam was *133 percent greater* than on the class mark.
- BC First Nations Studies: Failure rate on the exam was *150 percent greater* than on the class mark.
- English 12: Failure rate on the exam was *300 percent greater* than on the class mark.
- English 12 First Peoples: Failure rate on the exam was *1000 percent greater* than on the class mark.
- Communications 12: Failure rate on the exam was *125 percent greater* than on the class mark.

This pattern was relatively consistent over a period of five years, and it *demonstrates how low teachers' standards are in requiring minimum competencies for passing these courses.*

At the other end of the scale, British Columbia groups together students, when reporting to the public, who receive marks C+, B, *and* A, rather than just the more traditional approach of high scholarship—i.e., A. This approach is a concern, because it masks to the public what is happening at the highest level, where the "arms race for A marks" is the greatest. Nevertheless, with such a broad category of marks, these class marks of C+, B, and A from the classroom teacher always surpassed British Columbia's provincial test marks.

- English 10: 28 percent *greater* on the class mark.
- Math 10 (Precalculus): 19 percent *greater* on the class mark.
- Math 10 (Applied): 225 percent *greater* on the class mark.
- Science 10: 19 percent *greater* on the class mark.
- Social Studies 11: 14 percent *greater* on the class mark.
- Civic Studies 11: 30 percent *greater* on the class mark.
- BC First Nations Studies: 63 percent *greater* on the class mark.
- English 12: 27 percent *greater* on the class mark.
- English 12 First Peoples: 31 percent *greater* on the class mark.
- Communications 12: 6 percent *greater* on the class mark.

British Columbia and Alberta are the two Canadian provinces most successful on international PISA tests; yet their students receive, from teachers, classroom marks that are consistently and substantially inflated. We believe this is an accurate statement, because students write the same provincial tests that are carefully constructed by testing experts and then marked by professionals who have no knowledge about the writer. When marks on these tests are consistently lower on every subject over many years, the pattern confirms that classroom teachers are being influenced by factors not related to students' actual knowledge of curriculum outcomes.

It is noteworthy that these provincial tests come in grade levels *after the international PISA tests are written.* Regional research demonstrates that levels of student achievement decline in schools when higher rates of grade inflation are evident. Students receive the message that they are doing well in their studies when they receive inflated marks from their classroom teachers, and they then spend less time preparing for their end-of-year examinations.

The problem evident in these higher marks from classroom teachers reveals a *blind spot* within the education system. A logical pattern would be more in line with zero-sum, in which comparisons between class and system tests would even out. Instead, the common pattern that class marks are almost always higher than marks recorded on system tests reveals that *a relationship between a teacher and his or her student culminates in higher grades.* This grade inflation means that classroom standards are too low.

This chapter demonstrates how two high-performing school systems experienced unacceptable levels of grade inflation from the classroom teachers. Most jurisdictions across North America have lower levels of student learning, as recorded by PISA tests, which are well below these two Canadian provinces, yet the final marks awarded by their classroom teachers rival those in these provinces.

For example, Canada also utilizes a national testing program—the Pan-Canadian Assessment Program—which incorporates student surveys. When asked for the marks received from their classroom teachers, Alberta, which was the highest-performing province that year, had the fewest students reporting a mark higher than 70 percent. The *blind spot* with teachers is their *continued use of the bell curve (see chapter 5), rather than assessing learning against grade-level standards.*

Overcoming this tendency to adopt a bell-curve mentality is an important issue in the debate across the United States regarding the controversial Common Core standards. Employing common standards of learning coupled with common assessments consistently across the states would expose situations in which poor teaching and inadequate learning situations have been covered up by merely giving students high marks. Politicians will be shocked by reality when student learning is assessed consistently and they are required to defend results that are below normal expectations.

The next chapter documents how pervasive grade inflation is throughout the world of education. It is also important to note the absence of research that contradicts this generalization. Finally, the story does not end with only the conclusion that classroom assessment suffers from low standards, but chapter 6 will document an even greater tragedy: that *grade inflation is not equally applied across all students* within classrooms.

THE KEY POINTS MADE IN THIS CHAPTER ARE:

- Classroom assessments in two high-performing Canadian provinces—Alberta and British Columbia—are considerably higher than marks on provincial tests at both ends of the achievement scale.
- Grade inflation is an appropriate description when class marks are consistently higher than marks on standardized tests that utilize anonymous markers.
- Grade inflation exposes the teacher tendency to apply a bell-curve philosophy more than to apply standards of learning.

Chapter 5

Teachers' Inconsistency When Assessing Students

Evaluating students' work is a major activity in teaching. While it is also a legislated requirement, teachers naturally understand the value in constantly assessing student learning so that they can give feedback to the student, report to parents on their child's learning, report to the public on the extent of learning in general, and use the assessments to modify future instruction. Assessment is so critical to the educational process that a teacher's skill in evaluating student achievement requires constant verification and ongoing honing in practice.

Teachers' unions' orchestrated efforts to discredit large-scale testing make it necessary to openly discuss this issue. Their active insistence that teachers' marks on student learning are accurate must be verified so that trust is deserved. If the evidence refutes such accuracy, then trust must be replaced with accountability. This chapter further challenges teachers' capacity to perform consistently accurate assessments of student achievement.

Richard Phelps, in 2008, addressed a world congress on student evaluation and clearly expressed his findings with these words:

> There is abundant evidence that teachers' marks are a very unreliable means of measurement. A teacher's grades and test scores are far less likely to be generalizable than any standardized tests. If any assessment system uses tests that are not standardized, the system is likely to be unfair to many candidates. We (educators) need standardized tests because each of us is a prisoner of our own limited experiences and observations.

Phelps opens the Pandora's box by referencing the likelihood for *unfairness* in teacher assessments. Using this term to describe inconsistencies in marking typically provokes a significant backlash from teachers' unions. Criticism of teachers' evaluation skills is one thing, but to suggest that it results in *unfairness toward students* is something the unions want kept under wraps. Experienced educators likely understand the veracity of Phelps's statement that they are a "prisoner of [their] own limited experiences and observations." Seldom do teachers observe each other in the classroom, exchange their students' tests and compare assessments, or participate in marking centers in which student anonymity is ensured.

The stakes for the teaching profession are high if issues of inconsistency and bias are revealed. Inconsistent evaluations of student achievement recently surfaced as a major concern in the United Kingdom. Teachers' unions were pressuring their UK government to abandon large-scale testing in favor of trusting teachers' capacity to accurately assess students' achievements. The government established an expert panel to review the issue, and Bevan et al. (2009) recorded the panel's response to the request with the following statement:

> A high level of accountability for each school is beneficial for everyone who has a stake in the education system: pupils, parents, schools and the taxpayer. The fact that we have strong accountability in the education system means that we can confidently devolve a lot of autonomy to schools and invest high levels of trust in teachers and school leaders. It would therefore be misguided to weaken accountability.
>
> The accuracy and consistency of teacher assessment is improving; and whilst there are issues around variability of marking in tests, independently measuring pupils against national standards remains, in our view, the best way of providing objective information on the performance of each pupil and each school.

The implication in this report is that *trust follows accountability*. Blind trust is not useful to anyone, and therefore, measuring pupils against national standards is best achieved by using an assessment independent from the students' own schools.

In the United States, consistency in evaluating student work is a longstanding concern. An entry on school grading systems in the *Gale Encyclopedia of Education* traced the root of concern regarding marking inconsistencies back to the beginning of the twentieth century. As more children remained in school beyond grade 5, a shift to percentage grading seemed a natural byproduct for increased numbers of students. Inconsistent marks on assessments quickly became a concern.

This encyclopedia references a study in 1912 by Daniel Starch and Edward Elliott, in which teachers marked up identical English papers. On the first paper, the range of marks was from 64 percent to 98 percent, with a second paper ranging from 50 percent to 97 percent. These findings precipitated a similar study for mathematics, which demonstrated an even greater discrepancy, with marks ranging from 28 percent to 95 percent. It was evident from these early studies that teachers were applying a variety of *personal biases* while marking these student papers.

These discrepancies that were evident when assigning marks to the same answers led to another methodology for reporting, which made use of scales with larger ranges, such as excellent, average, poor, and failing. This shift to ranges in marks was also the genesis for using the letter grades A, B, C, D, and F. While these methods reduced variation in grades from the earlier practice of percentages, they still did not resolve the problem of teacher subjectivity. These ranges merely masked discrepant marks that were less than twenty to twenty-five percentage points.

ASSESSMENT INCONSISTENCIES AND THE BELL CURVE

Combating these problems led to the introduction of the *bell curve, with its prescribed distribution of scores for each of the letter grades.* This *quota system* for each letter grade, also known as "grading on the curve," relieved teachers of the difficult task of having to identify specific learning criteria for each mark range. The focus was on *ranking* students, rather than on *rating* their students' learning relative to preset standards. In other words, teachers found it relatively easier to place students' papers in a *rank order*, from best to poorest.

Teachers could readily discern differences in the quality of assignments turned in from students within their class and, not having to apply standards, could assess each student's response relative to the others'. The difficulty teachers had experienced was in assigning a value to the work that would be applied consistently by all teachers across the state, school district, or even within their own school. Over time, teachers might eventually develop an understanding of expectations for a specific grade and stray away from using the quota approach. When this occurred, inconsistencies were magnified, because some teachers applied the quota while others focused on the standards.

Unfortunately, subjectivity always remained an issue. The *Gale Encyclopedia* states:

Negative consequences result when subjectivity translates to bias. This occurs when factors apart from students' actual achievement or performance affect their grades. Studies have shown, for example, that cultural differences among students, as well as their appearance, family backgrounds, and lifestyles, can sometimes result in biased evaluations of their academic performance. Teachers' perceptions of students' behavior can also significantly influence their judgments of academic performance. Students with behavior problems often have no chance to receive a high grade because their infractions overshadow their performance. These effects are especially pronounced in judgments of boys. Even the neatness of students' handwriting can significantly affect teachers' judgments.

This tendency toward bias and its negative result on students is the purpose for this chapter and the reason that large-scale testing and anonymous marking are necessary for a fair approach in assessing student achievement. When unfairness is detected, actions designed to ensure fairness must follow.

ASSESSMENT INCONSISTENCIES TODAY

After a century of dealing with the problem of subjectivity in assessment, it remains a dominant issue in education. Webber et al. (2009) summarize their findings:

> Student assessment is a contested educational issue in most of the Western world.... Teachers' weak understanding of fair assessment practices appears to be a barrier to student assessment being perceived as a positive educational endeavor.... Reporting to stakeholders clearly, accurately, and sensitively is among the most difficult and uncomfortable parts of student evaluation for teachers and, therefore, may result in student achievement not being reliably conducted, interpreted or reported.... Much research suggests that teachers in general are not proficient in student assessment practices in the western world.... Further, principals are not strong in leading assessment and assessment historically has been missing from principal preparation programs.

Assessment is so critical in education, and yet it remains so poorly done, that professional development conferences for upgrading skills flourish. Bob Marzano, an assessment guru, demonstrated the extent of this issue at a conference involving two thousand educators in Atlanta, Georgia, on October 19, 2007. After posting on the screen a student's marks for ten assignments, he requested a final letter grade from conference participants. Amazingly, the range was from 30 percent to 90 percent, providing a clear indication that inconsistency remains a significant barrier to fairness for students.

Jost (2002) compared the relationship of course grades to a standardized test score that was comparable across all schools, districts, and states. Data used in this study included public high-school student records from one diverse state in the continental United States, along with corresponding exam score records from the College Board. The conclusion was: "When comparing schools, it is not uncommon to see that *despite seemingly equal grades*, scores on achievement tests show great differences in the student populations." *Different assessment criteria are at play in classrooms than in standardized tests.*

Harlen (2004) also undertook a systematic review of research on the reliability of teachers' assessment used for summative purposes. He concluded that "the findings of the review by no means constitute a ringing endorsement of teachers' assessment; there was evidence of low reliability and bias in teachers' judgements." These biases lead to unfair treatment of students, because marks are their currency for obtaining scholarships and entry into universities. *Ultimately, students are winners or losers because of their teachers' specific biases.*

Craft, a retired teacher focused on assessment, blogged on September 24, 2014, that

> the business of determining student grades—whether on assessments or for final evaluations—has always been problematic…. Absolute objectivity is not possible when humans are involved. To improve learning, teachers need to improve uniformity in what they do as compared with what other teachers do.

Uniformity, or consistency, when teachers mark students' work remains a significant concern. In a regional study, consistency between teachers' assessments of student responses while marking provincial examinations was always monitored. Controls in place for these marking sessions ensured student anonymity and that each question was marked by two teachers. When their marks varied by more than one point on a five-point scale, a third marker would be involved.

Extensive training took place prior to the marking process, and markers took a break from their task *twice daily* to review their standards by scoring a "reliability review" paper. The group compared individual assessments and discussed reasons for mark variances. The commitment for achieving consistency *was well beyond* what occurred within any school, because scholarships and placement into prestigious university programs were at stake.

Yet still, even when there was so much effort expended toward achieving consistency in assessing students' written responses, approximately 25 percent of upper-stream English, 12 percent of upper-stream social studies, and 10 percent of chemistry questions had marks that required a *third read*—i.e., more than one mark difference on a five-mark scale. While third reader rates occurred less frequently for lower-stream courses, where stakes for students were somewhat lower, these studies, replicated with similar results during every examination period over several years, reveal how difficult it is to achieve consistency in student assessment.

Humans will always experience factors that expose their fallibilities. Their ability to concentrate may be disrupted by fatigue, hunger, noise, and emotional distractions in their lives. Interestingly, technology is advancing to the degree that computers can now be "trained" to mark students' papers without experiencing any of these distractions—and they can mark around the clock while humans sleep.

This region conducted numerous studies comparing computer and teacher marks, with amazing results. The most recent study, reported by Sands in the May 24, 2014, *Edmonton Journal*, stated, "A computer could do a better job than a teacher in marking grade 12 diploma exam essays…. [The grading software company's] automated algorithms outperformed human reliability in the study by about 20 percent." Perhaps society's gradual move toward automated vehicles will be the impetus to trust technology when marking students' tests.

Technology is already used routinely to replace humans in marking short-answer questions on tests, yet marking students' *essay answers* via computer may be too controversial for some. For this reason, school systems using assessment technology tend to resort to a two-marker approach, where one is a teacher and the other is a computer program. A third teacher provides the additional read when the first two markings reveal a discrepancy. In the final analysis, *providing a fair mark to students is what really matters, even though technology is involved.*

Conspicuous by its absence in educational research is any evidence that there is consistency in assessment. Educators and their unions are unable to counter concerns regarding assessment inconsistencies. Until there is evidence that students' work is measured accurately and consistently across the educational system, trust requires a *checks-and-balances* approach, such as is provided through *large-scale standardized assessment accompanied by anonymous marking.* Teachers' unions need to abandon their self-serving agendas, in favor of fairness to students, and politicians need to support students rather than pander to the teachers' unions.

Teacher preparation programs are not ameliorating the problem. In the regional studies, new teachers indicate preparedness for assessing student work as their greatest concern. And once these teachers enter the school system, they are confronted with their weakness. In regions not using standardized testing, there is less likelihood of teacher marks facing any sustained challenge from parents. The advent of standardized testing has altered the landscape, and now significant sums of taxpayer funding to school districts are designated toward teacher in-service training on assessment. The problem is complex, however, and inconsistency remains.

ASSESSMENT INCONSISTENCY AND GRADE INFLATION

As has already been stated, teachers bring their biases to the assessment process. Inconsistency in assessment is the central issue, but it is exacerbated by a tendency toward grade inflation. We can identify this as *inflation*, because classroom marks assigned by teachers are *skewed upward rather than in both directions*. Teachers' bias toward inflation likely stems from their belief that the content was successfully taught; the teacher then assumes more from the students' answers than what should be credited. In other words, the teacher believes that what has been taught has been caught. This assumption is so pervasive that one superintendent opined that grade inflation in his district was not *endemic*, it was *pandemic*.

The Organisation for Economic Cooperation and Development, which administers the tri-annual PISA tests, published a report in 2012 that discussed grade inflation in the United States. Its conclusion was that, "while anecdotal evidence on grade inflation abounds, studies on grade inflation in secondary schools are scarce. The existing evidence signals that grade inflation is common and that, at least in the United States, it has been increasing since the 1990s."

This report raises the matter regarding the *paucity of research on grade inflation in secondary schools*. Avoiding unpleasant research about the school system is the natural disposition within a school system, and reinforcing the message that classroom teachers are adherents to low standards is troublesome to taxpayers, especially when their funding of education is already one of the highest in the world, as is the case with the United States. School administrators and their political overseers are loath to disclose information that might be embarrassing to their particular school systems, especially if other regions nearby are maintaining secrecy on the matter.

Problems emanating from inconsistent marking can also be somewhat muted when marks are raised and parents are given an unwarranted "rosy" picture of their children's academic progress. When messages sent home reflect high standings, everyone is happy. More important, there are no complaints. *The result, however, is that standards will decline until something— such as standardized test results—takes place to challenge the marking system.* For this reason, parents should give greater attention to standardized test results and request that these results be made available to them whenever they review their children's academic progress.

In the United Kingdom, a Durham University study concluded that an A grade in 2009 was actually equivalent to a C grade in the 1980s. According to the *Telegraph*, this shocking trend goes together with the "all must have prizes ethos that has dominated education ... for decades, to the detriment of academic excellence." The newspaper's summative statement was: "Such are the wondrous effects of the grade inflation that has become endemic in public examinations" ("A-Level Results" 2009).

Whether it is *endemic*, as suggested by the newspaper, or *pandemic*, as suggested by the superintendent, grade inflation is a serious problem, because it is *fraudulent*. Thomas and Bainbridge (1997) examined many American

SCHOOL	SAT	Norm Referenced Test (%ile) Reading	Norm Referenced Test (%ile) Math	GRADE POINT
A	750	35	26	3.6
B	900	40	42	3.2
C	990	48	48	2.8
D	1050	58	55	2.6
E	1125	67	74	2.5

Figure 5.1   Comparing External Test Scores and Grade Point Averages

school districts and demonstrated how an inconsistent application in standards produces *unfairness*. In figure 5.1, the students from school "A" had the lowest marks of five schools on the SAT as well as on norm-referenced tests in the subjects of reading and math. Nevertheless, these same students had received high marks from their teachers, achieving a collective grade point average of 3.6.

The students from school "E" scored the highest of the five schools on the external tests, but they had the lowest grade point average. These authors summarized their overall findings with the following statement:

> It is extremely difficult to explain how the lowest achieving school can have a higher grade point average than the higher achieving schools. Yet, this same pattern is found in most of the school districts in which the authors have conducted School Effectiveness Audits.... The conclusion can be drawn that in low achieving schools with high-grade point averages, expectations are extremely low—just the opposite of what research indicates should be done. Having low expectations begets low achievement. The fraud is that the high-grade point average gives a false message to the students. Schools which expect little and provide high grades, regardless of the level of academic achievement, are fraudulent educational systems and should be corrected.

This summative conclusion may sound harsh when the term *fraud* is used; however, when the public is led to believe something that is beyond misleading and is actually false, how else should it be characterized? The report also reminds us that low achievement is the result of low expectations, because students are misled to believe they are doing well and that additional study time is unnecessary.

In 2008, the *Queen's Journal*, published at Queen's University in Ontario, Canada, demonstrated the extent of grade inflation throughout an entire province. Canada's *National Post* carried a story stating that the prestigious

McGill University "has become the first in Canada to insist applicants from Ontario have higher marks than their peers from other provinces to earn admission." Faced with increasing numbers of students seeking entry to a limited number of postsecondary placements, teachers endeavored to give their students an advantage in qualifying for entry by lowering their standards (see Dueck 2014).

McGill University acknowledged that students from Ontario were going to have their grades *deflated* by 7 percent to achieve greater fairness for students applying from other provinces. Ontario's abolition of province-wide exams decades earlier meant that the teacher's mark was then the final mark, and students registering with an A grade had increased from 18 percent in 1992 to 40 percent in 2007. The *Queen's Journal* editorial piece concluded that "the number of A-students isn't growing because people are getting smarter. Rather, academic standards have declined so it is easier to get an A than ever before—a phenomenon known as grade inflation" (Woods 2008).

In this 2008 report, James Côté, a sociology professor at the University of Western Ontario, explained that grade inflation creates an education system that hurts students.

> It differentiates among students less and gives them less feedback on the quality of work. It's generally a disincentive for working harder because it really means it's easier to get a higher grade. For the students who deserve the higher grade in the first place it can be demoralizing.... It also gives people false feedback that they themselves are above average. They get an inflated view of themselves in terms of who they are and what they can do academically.

He went on to state, "Standardized testing would help curb the problem.... We're hesitant [to use standardized tests] in Canada, but it would help."

Of course standardized tests would help! As stated in my previous book, *Education's Flashpoints*, Wikipedia researchers summarized their assessment of this issue by stating:

> In 2007, 40 percent of Ontario high school graduates leave with "A" averages—8 times as many as would be awarded in the traditional British system. In Alberta, as of 2007, just over 20 percent of high school graduates leave with an "A" average. This discrepancy may be explained by the fact that all Alberta high school students must write province-wide standardized exams, Diploma exams, in core subjects, in order to graduate.

Canada's University of Saskatchewan conducted a follow-up study in 2011. They found that high-school students from Alberta did better in their first year at that university than their peers from British Columbia, Manitoba, Ontario, or Saskatchewan did. The study followed twelve thousand incoming students over three years and found that the Alberta students' grades dropped

6.4 percentage points in their first year at the university, while students from the four other provinces saw a decrease of 19.6 percentage points.

Alberta is the only one of these five provinces that mandates diploma examinations. *By using provincial examinations, Alberta's educational system is able to limit the amount of grade inflation in its schools.* There still is evidence that grade inflation occurs and that it is significant, but their checks-and-balances approach provides for greater accuracy and consistency in assessing students' work.

The University of Saskatchewan report concluded that the "study also confirms what many of us in admissions suspected or knew anecdotally—grade inflation is common and the best students come from Alberta high schools." A reporter from the *Calgary Herald* (November 29, 2011) referenced this study, along with Dr. McQuillan, the University of Calgary's dean of arts, who said, "As admissions become more difficult and competitive, each school in Ontario tends to say, let's give our students a leg up by giving them higher grades.... There's an arms race of As going on" (McClure 2011).

While Ontario universities were loath to admit it publicly, for fear of creating controversy, registrars told McQuillan that they were *quietly adjusting the marks for Alberta students to compensate*. A follow-up to this story appeared in the *Vancouver Sun* (Steffenhagen 2012), in which it was acknowledged that the University of British Columbia "adds two percentage points to the averages of students applying from Alberta because the grading system is tougher in that province." Michael Bluhm, UBC's associate director of undergraduate admissions, was quoted as saying:

> We recognize this difference when evaluating Alberta students for admission. I'll be clear to state that this is not a boost or benefit, per se, to Alberta students over BC students; rather an acknowledgment that the two grading systems are different. Alberta is the only province where we currently see valid and quantifiable data to warrant consideration in our admission decisions.

Alberta is the only Canadian province with a complete regimen of school-leaving examinations, and it therefore provides evidence of how standardized testing provides some control over teachers' propensity to lower standards in their classroom assessments.

While Alberta's students experienced less grade inflation than students from other provinces, grade inflation was still evident in their high schools. Figure 5.2 demonstrates an interesting phenomenon: The general portrayal in this chart *is replicated annually and in all subjects* where there are two course streams. In this case, Social Studies 30 is the upper-stream course leading to a university program, and it demonstrates consistently that the school marks from teachers were higher than the diploma examination marks, for both the Acceptable Standard, or passing, and the Standard of Excellence, or A grade.

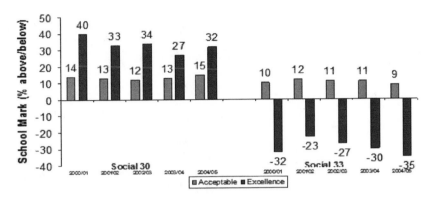

Figure 5.2   Diploma Examination Marks for Social Studies

For example, in the first year, listed at the chart's left edge, 14 percent more students achieved the Acceptable Standard and 40 percent more achieved the Standard of Excellence from their school than was earned on the diploma examination. This pattern of high discrepancies at the Standard of Excellence level is a second key aspect, important because it is at this standard that scholarships are won and placements in prestigious universities are achieved. Stakes are the highest at the Standard of Excellence level, and the consistency across the years is amazing and distributing.

Equally noteworthy is the pattern on the right-hand side of the chart, for the *lower-stream* Social Studies 33. Again, the variances between school-generated marks and diploma examination scores are consistent from year to year. There is, however, a strange pattern for the Standard of Excellence level here, because diploma examination marks are substantially below the school-generated marks. The explanation for this comes from interactions with many teachers of the lower-stream courses who indicated that they *do not give out A marks in lower-stream courses, because the student chose the easier stream.*

These teachers believed that students intentionally avoided the challenge of taking the more difficult stream of courses, and therefore, the teachers exercised *their own bias* in assessing student achievement by *penalizing them* for taking the easier course. In effect, *teachers completely disregarded course standards and applied their own.* Not only were these trends evident in social studies courses but they were replicated in the subjects of mathematics, English, and science. Inaccurate student assessments in the classroom were biased toward inflation—*except* when there was a perceived need to penalize students for not taking on coursework the teachers believed to be more challenging.

In a provincial meeting of school board trustees, an ex-teacher of Social Studies 33 took the podium and reiterated this *penalty aspect* to her colleagues. She openly acknowledged that she never gave an A to students in this course, because she felt that these students should have registered for the more challenging Social Studies 30. Even though students were demonstrating responses to examination questions at the A level, she intentionally imposed her own biases on her students by penalizing their choice in course load.

A final aspect of this Alberta study focused on what took place in each school district across the province. Again, the pattern was consistent from year to year, with only minor exceptions. Basically, in all school districts, *school-generated marks in upper-stream courses were higher than the students' diploma examination marks.* If this trend was not indicative of grade inflation, there would be a *relatively equal number of districts above and below this finding.* Diploma examinations may provide a checks-and-balances safeguard against some grade inflation, but elimination is not guaranteed; rather, diploma examinations only reduce the potential.

Upon reviewing these disturbing studies, one Alberta parent commented on how important it was to ensure consistent standards not only across the country *but also around the world.* She understood that registrars across Canada were adjusting student applicants' scores according to province, but what about students who were applying for university placement in other countries? Her child had applied to Harvard but had not been accepted. Defending fairness in an environment in which students' marks are highly inflated is difficult, because the degree of grade inflation is grossly unequal. There are winners and losers, and a teacher's sense of pride increases when his students experience the former.

Alberta's success at maintaining more consistent standards resulted in that parent's child receiving a more accurate set of marks, but this otherwise commendable state of affairs likely penalized her child, and presumably many others, who might otherwise have been accepted into a prestigious university located in another country unfamiliar with the high standards in that one Canadian province. For this reason, universities must be cognizant of student achievement whenever international testing, such as PISA, occurs, so that they can adjust acceptance standards, as demonstrated by the acceptance practices implemented by McGill University.

The interconnectedness of these studies on grade inflation within the educational system demonstrates the concern in Canada regarding fairness to students seeking entry into postsecondary institutions—both within Canada and internationally. Students should qualify for scholarships and gain entry to prestigious universities *because of merit based on achievement, rather than luck based on their location of residence.*

GRADE INFLATION LEADS TO LOWER
LEVELS OF STUDENT ACHIEVEMENT

Putting worthy students at a disadvantage is not the only unfair result of grade inflation, as Thomas and Bainbridge's earlier-referenced study points out. They found that students who received high grade point averages in their study of six schools had lower scores on the SAT and other standardized tests. Where grade inflation was the greatest, actual student achievement as measured by standardized assessments was the lowest.

Laurie (2007) undertook a similar study in Canada's maritime provinces located across the U.S. border north of America's "New England." His findings, subsequently replicated in regional research, found that in schools where students received marks most above their diploma examination scores, the examination scores were relatively the lowest in the test group. The opposite was also true: In schools where students experienced the least grade inflation, they had the relatively highest examination scores.

Students who receive inflated marks from their schools do not demonstrate similarly high levels of achievement on exit examinations, because *they suffer from a false sense of security*. They mistakenly believe they are doing well in their courses. Schools that expect little, yet provide high grades, regardless of the level of academic achievement, are purveyors of a fraudulent education that leaves parents and children believing something that is not true. Such action is unconscionable and should be exposed, confronted, and corrected.

One superintendent expressed her difficulty in adequately responding to a group of graduating students who had received high marks from their school but significantly lower marks on their final examinations. The university had advised these students, who had been provisionally accepted, that they had subsequently been rejected because the combined scores from their exams and from their teachers were too low. Dreams were shattered, and the superintendent—the most visible scapegoat—became the object of an outpouring of anger.

This pattern of grade inflation was evident year after year for many students in the same class. Students were lulled into apathy, or even worse, into visions of self-aggrandizement, by thinking they had "aced the course"; consequently, they were not diligent about preparing for their exams. In this specific instance, the superintendent had the uncomfortable task of informing the students and parents that nothing could be done except for them to retake the course next year.

This unfortunate incident illustrates the general inability of teachers to grade student achievement in an objective and accurate manner. Webber et al. (2009) summarized their interviews with secondary-school principals by stating that "secondary principals were not very positive about teacher

knowledge and practice in matters of fairness and equity and assessment."
Yet the stakes are high in secondary schools where scholarships are won and
entrances to prestigious universities are granted.

TEACHERS GRADUATE FROM A SYSTEM
PLAGUED BY GRADE INFLATION

High-school educators may excuse this tendency to inflate grades by pointing
out that grade inflation is rampant in universities, as well. Teachers come out
of an education system where marks below a B seldom occur and failure is
virtually nonexistent. Koedel (2011) analyzed major academic departments
at universities and reported how education marks are skewed upward. (See
figure 5.3.) Grade point averages for students enrolled in the education
department, and depicted in the line graph with the apex at the far right, were
much higher than they were in any other department.
    Koedel found that

> students who take education classes at universities receive significantly higher
> grades than students who take classes in every other academic discipline. The
> higher grades cannot be explained by observable differences in student quality
> between education majors and other students, nor can they be explained by the
> fact that education classes are typically smaller than classes in other academic
> departments. The remaining reasonable explanation is that the higher grades in
> education classes are the result of low grading standards. These low grading
> standards likely will negatively affect the accumulation of skills for prospective
> teachers during university training. More generally, they contribute to a larger
> culture of low standards for educators.... While all other university departments
> work in one space, education departments work in another.... The data consis-
> tently show that education departments award exceptionally favorable grades to
> virtually all their students in all their classes.

Babcock (2010) indicates that *grade inflation is associated with reduced
student effort* in college: put simply, students in classes where it is easier
to get an A do not work as hard. He demonstrated that in classes where the
expected *grade point average* rises by one point, students respond by reducing their effort, as measured by study time, *by at least 20 percent*. The implication for education degrees, therefore, is that *teachers who are being trained
actually know less because their marks are so high.*
    Using the data from figure 5.3, Koedel estimates that "if the grading stan-
dards in each education department were moved to align with the average
grading standards at their respective universities, student effort would rise

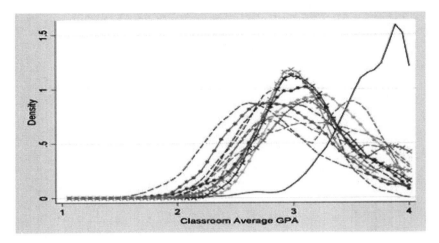

Figure 5.3   Comparison of Students' Grades across University Departments

by at least 11 to 14 percent." Koedel provides a hypothesis regarding why education departments and their deplorably skewed results escape detection:

> One notable difference between education departments and other major departments at universities is that virtually all graduates from education departments move into a single sector of the labor market—education. If the education sector is less effective at identifying low-quality graduates than are other sectors of the labor market, this would help explain why professors in education departments are able to consistently award As to most students.

Most university departments serve a diverse market. For example, the business department seeks to place graduates into an array of firms that can easily discern the differences in the quality of graduates from another institution. *Firms would cease hiring from lower-quality programs, forcing instructors to recalibrate their standards.* Education, on the other hand, is a closed system. Graduates are generally employed locally by the school board, which participates in the fostering of a culture of low standards. Like the university's department of education, the local school district is reticent to distinguish good teachers from mediocre teachers.

We have also pointed out that accountability in postsecondary education is out of balance and skewed when it relies on student satisfaction surveys. Over time, academic grades for work of comparable quality have increased, in what is known as the "standards creep." It appears that education department faculties also suffer from the low expectations of their students, who, in turn, eventually work with our children to prepare them for the "real world."

GRADE INFLATION IS HIGHEST FOR
THE HIGHER ACHIEVERS

Christina Wall (2003) proposes another reason for rampant grade inflation following her investigation that concluded by saying, "Grade inflation is prominent in most schools today. Perhaps it is due to the emphasis on morale. It could also be due to the emphasis of having good grades in order to get into good colleges and become successful." Wall's research and conclusion is generalizable throughout the literature, but it begs the question as to *why it occurs in elementary and middle school as well.* Students at these grade levels do not need a "leg up" to gain entry into a prestigious university program.

In the regional study, students wrote system-wide tests in grades 3, 6, and 9. These were low-stakes tests, and teachers were encouraged to mark their students' written responses as a first read or as a preliminary reading before the school forwarded the tests to a marking center *where anonymity was ensured.* This process enabled the province to study the impact that a teacher-student relationship had on the grade a student received. *Specifically, the student's teacher and an anonymous teacher marked the same piece of work; the study sought to determine whether there were differences and, if so, what the trend might be.*

The first phase of this study took five years, and it demonstrated a consistent result for each year and at each grade of the tests. At the Acceptable Standard, up to 8 percent more students achieved a "pass" from their classroom teachers than from the anonymous markers. At the Standard of Excellence, 86 percent more students received an A-level mark from their classroom teachers than from the anonymous markers. Because grade inflation in the classroom was so dramatic at the upper achievement levels, a meeting with superintendents was held to discuss the problem.

Superintendents were loath to undertake any action to ameliorate the problem. Large-scale testing was contentious, and acknowledging these significantly different results in marks was thought to be inflammatory and would likely lead to a backlash from union members, who at that time included the school principals. In the five years that followed, 79 percent more students still received the Standard of Excellence marks from their classroom teachers than from the marking centers, where student anonymity was tightly controlled. *Teachers' inconsistent marking is a problem made more worrisome from their tendency to inflate student scores, especially scores at the upper levels.*

Unfortunately, grade inflation, which unfairly disadvantages and advantages students, is not the only malevolent feature in the marking process. Subjectivity can seriously distort academic achievement, as the triennial

Canadian national testing program, Pan Canadian Assessment Program (PCAP), demonstrates. This program includes extensive surveying, which provides a context in which we can assess the nature of various relationships associated with student achievement.

One survey question asked teachers whether they incorporated *improvement* over a period of time when they assigned letter grades related to achievement. In other words, were students' final marks on how well they could divide influenced by how much they had improved since the beginning of the term? Teachers who responded affirmatively in the different provinces ranged from 13 percent to 72 percent. A second year, but with a different subject and different teachers responding to the same question, indicated a range of 13 percent to 66 percent. These variations demonstrate how assessments of student achievement can vary across provinces, yet they are consistent across teaching regardless of subject.

Another survey question focused on *attendance*, asking whether students' marks were influenced by this issue. Presumably students were penalized with lower marks if they were absent an inordinate number of days. On this issue, teachers from various jurisdictions varied in their responses from 6 percent to 66 percent. As with the previous question, these high and low responses were not significant outliers. In other words, other jurisdictions were also spread out across the range, with several relatively near to both ends of the scale.

Teachers were also asked whether or not their assessment of a student was influenced by his or her *participation* during class activities. Participation is a desired student behavior, but is it indicative of student learning in curriculum outcomes? Once again teachers varied widely in their attitudes, with as few as 12 percent saying it was an influence in some districts and as many as 63 percent saying it was an influence in others.

Improvement over time, attendance, and class participation are all qualities associated with being a good student. Parents usually want to know how their child is doing in these areas, because these are good predictors of how well their child will later perform in the workplace. However, should these qualities be conflated into an indication of a "good student," when the grade is intended to measure *competency* in a skill or the mastery of a concept? Logic suggests that it would be more truthful and more helpful if these valuable qualities were assessed independently and reported elsewhere.

The confusion on this issue opens the door to *inconsistency in assessment* and, therefore, *unfairness toward a segment of the student population*. If these or any other criteria such as behavior, status in the class, cleanliness, or neatness are considered when reporting achievement in a subject, teacher bias has been introduced.

INCORPORATING NON-ACADEMIC FACTORS
INTO ACHIEVEMENT REDUCES SUCCESS

For these non-academic factors, it is noteworthy that Alberta was at the lowest end of the scale on three of the survey questions (including the two years when improvement was the focus), and within 3 percent from the bottom on the fourth. Yet this province persistently recorded the *lowest percentage of teacher assessments* for Canadian students, with a mark of 70 percent or higher. In other words, *Alberta students had the lowest set of class marks from teachers across the entire country, while having the lowest percentage of teachers conflating marks for learning with behavior.*

At the same time, this province repeatedly scored the *highest* on national and international assessments. The applicable generalization is that the jurisdiction with the strictest adherence to marking relative to standards, and the least likelihood of subjectivity leading to bias and grade inflation, also had the highest levels of student achievement as measured on standardized tests.

In 2007, a report from the Canadian Ministers of Education (CMEC) assessed the impact of teachers' comingling of attendance, participation, effort, improvement, and behavior with students' scores in reading achievement. Figure 5.4 demonstrates that on each criterion, students' test marks were significantly lower when the teacher included consideration of the criterion than when it was not considered.

For example, students with teachers who indicated they did not include *attendance* in their students' marks scored an average of 495 on their reading achievement test. Students whose teachers indicated they did include *attendance* scored some thirty points lower on the achievement test. In each instance, using a non-academic factor yielded a lower result in this national assessment of reading.

It is apparent, therefore, that teachers who are prone to incorporating non-academic criteria do their students a disservice, because including these biases leaves students with an inflated understanding of their learning. They thus experience a disincentive to work harder. In simple language, *teachers are disadvantaging their students by not confining their marks to what their students learned.*

While Alberta's students benefited from assessment based on standards, this benefit evaporated when the province's school boards began importing many of their teachers from the rest of Canada to accommodate a class-size reduction program and the retirement of a significant number of teachers. The national testing program's survey registered an immediate change in the degree to which Alberta teachers utilized *non-academic factors* in assigning final marks for their students.

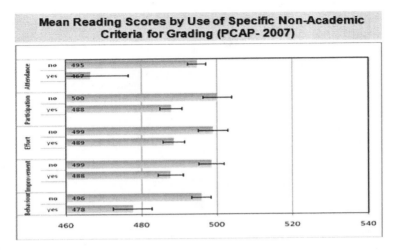

Figure 5.4 Examining Specific Non-Academic Criteria in Grading

Previous national studies had routinely demonstrated that Alberta teachers were relatively averse to using non-academic factors, but with the influx of new teachers, the scores ballooned to the point that 64 percent of Alberta's teachers indicated they were now employing such an approach to grading.

Webber et al.'s follow-up study (2009) in Alberta determined that teachers "always" or "often" used factors such as:

- Penalties for late assignments (33 percent)
- Adjustment of grades to recognize student behavior (17 percent)
- Adjustment of grades to recognize neatness (11 percent)
- Adjustment of grades based on student attendance (6 percent)
- Bonus marks for extra work accomplished (35 percent)

This study went on to ask students whether or not they felt teachers assessed a variety of factors in addition to academic achievement when they were given a score in a subject. The results affirmed that this was the case. In their minds, their grades had been adjusted for the following reasons:

- Report card marks were changed because of late assignments (87 percent agreed).
- Grades were adjusted to recognize student behavior (47 percent of secondary students and 70 percent of elementary students agreed).
- Grades were adjusted because of how neatly the work was done (31 percent of secondary students and 69 percent of elementary students agreed).
- Bonus marks for extra work were given (48 percent agreed).

A summary statement from the researchers indicated that "secondary students admonished that the system is for teachers, not students and that teacher bias is a real problem. Students who are favored get better marks.... Grades are reduced for misbehavior, and if a student is disruptive then grades go down."

Concurrently a significant shift occurred in the province-wide diploma examination marks. We have already indicated that system-wide examination marks are always lower than school-generated marks. So predictable is this outcome that only rarely do any of the sixty-two school districts record an average examination mark that is higher than that assigned by teachers. Despite the province's outstanding success on the world stage of international testing, grade inflation still occurred, albeit to a lesser degree than in any other Canadian jurisdictions.

During a three-year period of extensive teacher hiring and turnover, grade inflation increased dramatically. At the beginning of this three-year period, only *three* districts had a variance greater than 10 percent between the average school and examination marks for English. But three years later, *seventeen* districts *exceeded* the 10 percent threshold; this occurred even though *provincial examination marks* demonstrated a *significant decline*.

In mathematics, this threshold was *exceeded* by only *five* districts at the beginning of the study, but it increased to *eighteen* districts by the conclusion of Webber et al.'s study. The significant increase in school-generated marks was not matched by a similar gain in learning on the provincial exit examination. In the initial year of this study, 83 percent of students met the examination's Acceptable Standard; three years later, it remained essentially the same (82 percent).

The same was true with the Standard of Excellence: Over the three-year period, the decline was inconsequential. Because these exams are now set to be equal in difficulty from year to year, all that changed was the teacher-generated mark, which increased significantly and reflected a new interpretation of the standards.

During this period, another disturbing story emerged from surveys of employers that the province conducted. Their satisfaction with graduates' skills and the quality of their work plummeted to their lowest level, with a decline from 77 percent satisfaction to 67 percent. Such a dramatic decline had never occurred before, which raised concerns about a growing mismatch between the teachers' ability to assess students' achievement and the employers' need to hire skilled workers. This variation between classroom marks and employer perceptions provided another indication that grade inflation within the classroom was increasing.

Introducing non-academic factors into the assessments of student achievement produced significant grade inflation at a time when national and international assessments indicated that actual student achievement was declining. Meanwhile, class size reduction, which was purported to improve the learning environment, required the province to increase the number of teachers by 13 percent. Growth in enrollment and a wave of retirements associated with an aging workforce also drove up the number of new hires, many of whom were unfamiliar with the province's curricular standards. These factors coalesced to create a negative impact on student achievement.

A SIMPLE ILLUSTRATION OF HOW
GRADE INFLATION OCCURS

One more point needs to be made: The longitudinal data reveal how insidious grade inflation can be. Both the examination and school marks were based on percentages, and school marks were skewed significantly to the right. Because student test scores produced a normal distribution, we can be confident that test developers successfully differentiated students based on achievement.

School-generated marks, however, did not demonstrate a normal distribution, which means that factors other than student achievement were in play. For example, in one course required for university entrance, more than three times as many students received a mark of 80 percent than those recorded in the examination. At 90 percent, it was doubled, and school marks were significantly skewed upward beginning at 70 percent. There was another curious fact that strongly suggested the presence of human bias and predilection.

In our modern economy, we often "round up" or "round down" in an effort to make things simpler. In teacher-recorded marks, the study revealed a very discernible pattern of "rounding up" that would have had nothing to do with achievement. For example, there were many scores that ended in zeroes or fives—far more than would have been statistically expected. At the same time, there were disproportionately few grades recorded as X8 or X9.

It was determined that schools were systematically *bumping up marks* by one or two percentage points to qualify for a higher letter grade or scholarship. This rounding up was not compensated with a rounding down, and while this explains a minor portion of how grade inflation occurs, the story does not end there. Because the bump ups were not universally applied, so that fewer students received a mark ending in 8 or 9, we can assume that that some teachers and some schools took a different approach to assessment. In other words, some teachers did not round up marks for those students whose scores ended in X8 or X9.

Students in the schools that rounded up temporarily benefited, but other students did not. To what can we attribute this fundamental unfairness:

Gender? Compliant behavior? This question will be discussed, in part, later. The point here is that a pattern of unfairness does, in fact, exist in the system, and the evidence extends across all subjects and over many years. The application of certain biases was routinely practiced at the school level and contributed to the natural inclination toward grade inflation. Lower standards at the school level were the norm.

STUDENT CHEATING AND GRADE INFLATION

It is possible that concerns with grade inflation at the school level are compounded by a disconcerting problem that is frequently overlooked and often not even acknowledged. Cheating can profoundly inflate a student's grade, but it could be essentially eliminated on achievement tests if the school had followed prescribed protocols. Perhaps this issue is too disconcerting for educators to even acknowledge. If factual, student cheating can seriously jeopardize student fairness.

Academic cheating in postsecondary institutions is well documented. This is less so for the K-12 school system, although what we do know is equally disturbing. McCabe et al. (2001) studied high-school cheating involving 4,500 U.S. schools and found that:

- 74 percent of students admitted to *serious test cheating*.
- 72 percent admitted to serious cheating on written work.
- 97 percent admitted to copying homework or to test copying.
- 30 percent admitted to *repetitive* serious cheating on tests/exams.
- 15 percent had obtained a term paper from the Internet.
- 52 percent had copied at least a few sentences from a website without citing the source.

Unfortunately, the 2002 Report Card on the Ethics of American Youth determined that cheating was *on the rise*. Comparing their student survey results for 1992 and 2002, the percentage of students admitting that they had cheated on an examination had increased from 61 percent to 74 percent.

Newberger (1999) compared current data with that from the 1940s and found that in a 1997 survey of "high achievers" in high school, 87 percent judged cheating to be "common" among their peers. Seventy-six percent confessed that they themselves had cheated. By way of contrast, a national sample of U.S. college students in the 1940s found that only 20 percent admitted to cheating in high school *when they were questioned anonymously*. Cheating is considerably more prevalent today, and, contrary to some people's opinions, *cheating is not restricted to weak students attempting to improve their chances at passing.*

Niels (2014) researched the major reasons students cheat and published his results online on the website About.com. His research led him to believe that students cheated for the following reasons:

1. There is a mechanism within each of us that triggers a need to "save face." Saving face can mean a desire to save oneself from the angry assault of a parent or teacher.
2. Cheating is *no longer considered "deviant" behavior but "normal" behavior*, because "everybody does it."
3. Cheating offers an easy way out. Why bother studying hard and doing all those term papers by yourself if you can just use someone else's work?

Niels's findings support the notion that cheating can occur with students of *every ability level, whenever they see the need to get ahead without expending the necessary effort*. These findings also imply that the odds of being caught are relatively small.

Newberger also verifies that the odds of getting away with academic cheating are heavily skewed in the cheater's favor: "Ninety percent of the confessed cheaters surveyed by *Who's Who* said they had never been caught." The incentive has changed from passing, for the weak student, to getting into select universities, for the stronger students.

In the regional study, cheating on standardized, system-wide tests, where the process occurs under tight security, was very low, with an incidence rate of 1 percent whenever two or more students were detected as having the same pattern of answers. Invigilators systematically monitored the examination room; furthermore, students working on the same test were surrounded with open space and could be observed from multiple angles.

It is noteworthy that in the few instances when students did cheat, *they were writing tests they deemed to be of the greatest importance*. This included tests in subjects that were required for a graduation diploma and entrance into a chosen university. In other words, these students were the stronger ones, who were wishing to retain their places in the system and who would eventually enter prestigious university programs and pursue futures in well-paying jobs.

The reality of stronger students cheating to succeed in a competitive environment was corroborated by Davis et al. (2009), who said:

> It's not the dumb kids who cheat.... It's the kids with a 4.6 grade point average who are under such pressure to keep their grades up and get into the best colleges. They're the ones who figure out how to cheat without getting caught.... Grades are a commodity in our knowledge society and, with many students, they represent the end goal of schooling.

The goal of "saving face" in an environment that increasingly appears to view cheating as normal is observable in the lower grades. Bushway and Nash (1977) indicated that "academic dishonesty is endemic in all levels of education. In the United States, studies show that 20 percent of students started cheating in the first grade." Similarly, other U.S. studies reveal that 56 percent of middle school students admit to cheating (Decoo 2002).

Canadian researchers have not given as much attention to cheating as those in the United States. Nevertheless, the work that has been done reveals a pattern like that found in the United States. In 2006, the University of Guelph and Rutgers University surveyed fifteen thousand students and found that "73 percent of university students reported instances of serious cheating on written work while in high school."

The discussion on cheating has focused, thus far, on student behavior that is covert. There also is an overt form of cheating that might not even be referred to as cheating, because it is actually an encouraged activity. Davis et al. (2009) describes this activity, one that ends up giving some students an advantage over their peers: "Think of a student who receives 'help' from his parents on his science project or her essay. If a student is transparent about the assistance received, she might not receive as high a grade than if the teacher thinks the student did her assignment on her own." How frequently does *this* type of advantage occur?

Canada's PCAP national testing program asked thirteen-year-old students across the nation how frequently they worked with their parents on their homework. *Two out of three students* affirmed that they received assistance: 35 percent said it occurred a few times a month, 26 percent said it took place a few times a week, and 6 percent indicated that it happened almost daily. We likely experience some inner turmoil with any suggestion that this parental assistance is cheating; yet, if the teacher is not aware of it and is assessing the final product in any way, some students are more advantaged than others. Some are therefore disadvantaged. *Unfairness has occurred.*

These surveys also asked teachers to identify how frequently homework assignments were used in determining marks. Given that 44 percent indicated that such assignments were used to determine the final mark, it is apparent that some students were clearly advantaged by parental involvement, and that this advantage was a significant factor. Hopefully teachers are sufficiently astute to track the degree to which their students receive parental assistance. To the degree this monitoring does not occur, however, we can assume that grade inflation is translating as unfairness to students. Ryan (1998) references unfairness resulting from plagiarism, which is equally applicable to any unknown assistance:

> Often lost in the discussion of plagiarism is the interest of the students who don't cheat. They do legitimate research and write their own papers. They work

harder (and learn more) than the plagiarists, yet their grades may suffer when their papers are judged and graded against papers that are superior but stolen material. Students have a right to expect fairness in the classroom. When teachers turn a blind eye to plagiarism, it undermines that right and denigrates grades, degrees, and even institutions.

Many teachers and administrators understand how grade inflation occurs, because they admit students into their programs who struggle to learn, yet receive relatively high grades. Research evidence indicates that the assessment of student achievement is inconsistent, because various forms of bias find their way into a teacher's mind-set. As offensive as the phrase "unfairness to students" might be to some, any time students are advantaged or disadvantaged by these biases, the result is *unfair to some or all*. There is no merit in attempting to cloak the issue in secrecy, as so frequently occurs.

This issue of fairness has a parallel in professional golf. All players are responsible to monitor and, if necessary, to challenge their competitors' decisions when they are playing in the same group. The winner of a golf tournament is the player with the lowest score over several rounds. Because there are many groups of players and insufficient numbers of referees to observe each golfer, players are responsible to their fellow competitors in other groups to ensure that a competitor in their group is scoring by the rules. This practice is a check and balance for ensuring fairness for the field of golfers in the tournament. Golf may be an honorable sport, but trust has its limitations.

One focus in education should be that of *trust versus accountability*. Teachers want parents and the public to trust unquestioningly their assessments of student learning. Their unions understand that without large-scale testing, the entire accountability effort in the K-12 system collapses. Such an environment is like what exists in most postsecondary programs, where instructors use "academic freedom" to avoid accountability.

Sole discretion to determine the curriculum and the assessment of learning is the preferred situation for teachers' unions, which argue that every learning environment is unique and therefore nothing can be seen as being in common and capable of standardization. This leaves the classroom an impregnable fortress, in which the teacher—the monarch of the domain—rules benevolently without fear of accountability.

This is a scenario that cannot and will not survive. Public scrutiny today, born in part out of a growing awareness of the conclusions researchers are drawing from multiple longitudinal studies, makes it clear that the old methods must go. Trust will remain, but it will do so in a new and open context, in which respectful dialogue and a new attitude of cliental service emerges.

The global community is altering the K-12 system, because the advent of standardized testing now identifies which countries are providing higher levels of student learning. Results from these cyclical tests are like the sports environment, in which athletes come together every four years for contests. In the field of education, these tests are like an "Olympics of Learning," with one significant variation: Rather than involving elite athletes, as in sports, random samples of the general student population are involved in measuring educational standards. The focus, therefore, is on the average.

As in sports, in which countries undertake various initiatives to improve athletic performance, and thereby raise the bar of excellence for themselves and others, educational leaders today also feel the pressure to stay abreast of rising international standards. Strategies for improvement may come in the form of increased resources or accountability. The result is that politics, more than ever before, is involved with education, and when this occurs, politicians inevitably choose sides.

The message of this chapter is that "fairness to students" requires a checks-and-balances approach that features large-scale testing of student achievement with regard to established standards. The results leave students and their parents with an ability to judge for themselves how well the student is learning and to be confident that this measurement is a fair and accurate assessment of what it purports to measure.

This, in turn, creates the possibility of holding accountable those who are responsible for the learning environment. It is this measurement process that applies pressure on those within the educational system to improve their performance. *Reaction against this pressure is what produces the conflict that is now so evident in the politics of education.*

Teachers' unions need to reexamine their resistance to large-scale testing. The evidence of the teacher's inability to assess student achievement in a consistent and fair manner is overwhelming. To be fair to students, unions must become advocates of a new approach that puts the best interest of students first, while trusting that the welfare of teachers will be appropriately addressed. *As it now stands, unions are the most significant inhibitors of fairness to students.*

Politicians who are faced with this conflict must consider their ability to win their next electoral contest. Will they side with the unions, which could readily influence their members' votes? Will they side with students, who have limited understanding of fairness issues and cannot vote? To what extent will they release information to the public, so that they are more informed about the nature of the conflict? These are significant issues in educational politics, and it is necessary to draw politicians into the discussion so that their positions are clearly stated and publicly understood.

While we usually trust our service providers, it is folly to do so blindly. As Edward Deming once stated, "In God we trust; all others bring data." The data story in student assessment should provide our elected representatives with the evidence they need to take a public, persuasive stand that makes fairness to students the highest priority in their education platforms.

THE KEY POINTS MADE IN THIS CHAPTER ARE:

- Teachers' unions attempt to equate standardized testing with a lack of trust in their capacity to accurately assess students' work.
- "What we do for students, we should do for teachers" is a key leadership principle.
- Transparency is a new reality for teachers.
- Research verifies that teachers' marks are an unreliable means of measurement.
- The bell-curve philosophy regarding quotas emerged because of inconsistent marking.
- Assessment inconsistency is skewed toward grade inflation, which leads to fraudulent marks.
- Grade inflation produces complacency and lower results on students' end-of-year course examinations.
- Teachers' tendency toward inflating student grades may stem from their experience in teacher preparation programs, which produce highly inflated marks.
- Grade inflation is greatest at the high end of mark distributions.
- When non-academic factors are incorporated into a student's achievement marks, there is less likelihood of academic success.
- Grade inflation readily occurs in a percentage grading system, because teachers routinely "bump up" marks to a number ending in "5" or "0."
- Grade inflation also occurs because of increased levels of student cheating, which occurs more frequently at higher levels of achievement.

Chapter 6

Grade Inflation Is Not
Uniformly Evident

Grade inflation arising from low standards in our classrooms has been documented in the previous two chapters, and this problem is virtually universal across North America. *Numbers don't lie*, and the concern should be more than disconcerting: *It should be distressing.* There is no value to our society in giving *undeserved* credit to students or by *defrauding* taxpayers of the full value of their tax dollars. The greatest harm is perpetuated in our workforce, *which is developing a mind-set that considers maximum effort as being unnecessary.*

The inconsistent assessment of students' academic achievement has been a long-standing problem that is too frequently disregarded because the information has not been transparently presented for public scrutiny. While this lack of transparency is an issue, inflated marks are seldom disputed by students or their parents. This is especially so when the pattern shows that these high marks are not irregular "blips" but an ongoing problem throughout the school system.

This concern about low standards in the classroom focused, in chapter 4, on two Canadian provinces with high-achieving fifteen-year-old students, as measured by the 2015 PISA international assessments. Both British Columbia and Alberta classrooms in senior high schools demonstrated significantly consistent grade inflation in teachers' classroom marks when compared to their provincial test results. The broader view, presented in chapter 5, demonstrated how pervasive the problem is throughout educational systems. Not examined in these chapters, however, is whether grade inflation *occurred equally across all student populations*, which is the specific focus in this chapter.

GENDER UNFAIRNESS IN BRITISH COLUMBIA

A suitable means for beginning this chapter is a comment made by British Columbia when it responded to a request for information, specifically: "Provincial reports indicate a relatively high correlation between the classroom and exam marks across gender and do not suggest that classroom marks exhibit gender unfairness." However, an analysis of their 2015 school year results makes it difficult to corroborate this conclusion. Recall that this jurisdiction rolls up the higher-achieving marks, with C+, B, and A placed into one category.

- **English 10:** The advantage (scoring C+, B, or A) accorded to female students on the *exam* is 13 percent, but in *classrooms* it is 18 percent, or *plus 5 percent.*
- **Math 10 (Precalc):** The advantage (scoring C+, B, or A) accorded to female students on the exam is 1 percent, but in classrooms, it is 6 percent, or *plus 5 percent.*
- **Math 10 (App):** The advantage (scoring C+, B, or A) accorded to female students on the exam is minus 6 percent, but in classrooms, it is plus 3 percent, or *plus 9 percent.*
- **Science 10:** The advantage (scoring C+, B, or A) accorded to female students on the exam is 1 percent, but in classrooms, it is 9 percent, or *plus 8 percent.*
- **Social Studies 11:** The advantage (scoring C+, B, or A) accorded to female students on the exam is minus 1 percent, but in classrooms it is 13 percent, or *plus 14 percent.*
- **Civic Studies 11:** The advantage (scoring C+, B, or A) accorded to female students on the exam is minus 1 percent, but in classrooms, it is plus 18 percent, or *plus 19 percent.*
- **BC First Nations Studies:** The advantage (scoring C+, B, or A) accorded to female students on the exam is 10 percent, but in classrooms, it is 23 percent, or *plus 13 percent.*
- **English 12:** The advantage (scoring C+, B, or A) accorded to female students on the exam is 8 percent, but in classrooms, it is 12 percent, or *plus 4 percent.*
- **English 12 First Peoples:** The advantage (scoring C+, B, or A) accorded to female students on the exam is 18 percent, but in classrooms it is 24 percent, or *plus 6 percent.*
- **Communications 12:** The advantage (scoring C+, B, or A) accorded to female students on the exam is 3 percent, but in classrooms, it is 14 percent, *or plus 11 percent.*

In each subject, female students were given C+, B, or A class marks more frequently than their male counterparts—which is not the issue. Rather, comparing these class marks with the provincial examination marks reveals our concern that the former *always favor females* by a considerably larger percentage. We can conclude that some teacher bias occurs that consistently places males at a disadvantage whenever these assessments are used for awards, scholarships, and placement in university programs.

GENDER UNFAIRNESS IN ALBERTA

Chapter 4 of this book has already documented the extent to which classroom teachers inflate their students' grades, because of the prevalence of low standards in assessment. This chapter's focus is on answering the question of whether grade inflation is uniformly evident across students, *because unfairness, when applied equally to everyone, can still be considered "fair." Unfairness rears its ugly head when consistency is lacking.*

Alberta's student enrollment corresponds to that of a midsized state in the United States. Grade-12 students write provincial exit tests—diploma examinations—upon the conclusion of semesters in January and June. Marks on these examinations are combined with class marks from teachers, resulting in a final mark on the students' transcripts. An analysis for the Standard of Excellence and Acceptable Standard of 2016 marks based on gender follows, *and it records how many more female students than males achieved each standard. (A negative sign depicts males as having a higher percentage.)*

January results (see table 6.1) demonstrate how females were awarded more Standard of Excellence marks from their teachers in *every subject*;

Table 6.1 January 2016: Standard of Excellence (Equivalent to an A) (Example: In ELA 30-2, 67 percent more females received Excellence from their teacher. In the provincial exam, 26 percent more females received Excellence. The female advantage from their teachers' mark is 41 percent.)

Subject	School Mark	Diploma Exam	Female Advantage
ELA 30-2	67%	26%	41%
ELA 30-1	48%	53%	-5%
Math 30-1	8%	-5%	13%
Math 30-2	59%	50%	9%
Biology	5%	-4%	9%
Science	31%	27%	4%
Chemistry	2%	-7%	9%
Physics	13%	1%	12%
Social Studies 30-1	19%	-14%	33%
Social Studies 30-2	33%	-1%	34%

Table 6.2   June 2016: Standard of Excellence (Equivalent to an A)

Subject	School Mark	Diploma Exam	Female Advantage
ELA 30-2	63%	29%	34%
ELA 30-1	39%	20%	19%
Math 30-1	6%	-2%	8%
Math 30-2	40%	56%	-16%
Biology	3%	-7%	10%
Science	39%	9%	30%
Chemistry	0%	-15%	15%
Physics	15%	0%	15%
Social Studies 30-1	15%	-3%	18%
Social Studies 30-2	35%	-1%	36%

however, females outscored the males in only five tests on the standardized provincial examinations marked *anonymously*. The prevalence of high marks from classroom teachers provided females with an advantage in nine of the ten courses, and this advantage provided more opportunity for *awards, scholarships, and placement in university programs for these females.* The overall advantage for females with higher class marks was 15.9 percent.

June results (see table 6.2) demonstrate how females were awarded more Standard of Excellence marks from their teachers in *every subject*; however, females outscored the males in only five tests on the standardized provincial examinations marked *anonymously*. The prevalence of high marks from classroom teachers provided females with an advantage in nine of the ten courses, and this advantage provided more opportunity for *awards, scholarships, and placement in university programs for these females.* The overall advantage for females from higher class marks was 16.9 percent.

Combining the January and June test administrations reveals that female students were awarded more Standards of Excellence in nineteen of the twenty *classroom assessments*: June's chemistry course was the exception, with 0 percent of female advantages recorded. However, using the system's diploma examinations, females and males had an equal number of test administrations, with the higher percentage scoring Standard of Excellence. Examining the upper-stream courses that are most important for university placement applications, males outscored females at the Standard of Excellence on eight of the twelve administrations.

January results (see table 6.3) demonstrate how females were *failed* less frequently by their teachers in every subject; however, females were failed at a higher percentage on three of the *standardized provincial examinations that were marked anonymously*. When class marks and provincial tests are viewed side by side, the third column demonstrates how much more females are advantaged, due to the large discrepancies between the two types of assessments.

Table 6.3 January 2016: Not Achieving the Acceptable Standard (Did *not* meet and therefore must retake the course)(Example: In ELA 30-2, 95 percent *more males* were assessed as "failed" from their teachers. In the provincial exam, 13 percent more males failed. The female advantage from the school mark is that 82 percent fewer girls failed, or almost double.)

Subject	School Mark	Diploma Exam	Female Advantage
ELA 30-2	-95%	-13%	82%
ELA 30-1	-110%	-8%	102%
Math 30-1	-42%	-1%	41%
Math 30-2	-67%	-36%	31%
Biology	-9%	4%	13%
Science	-92%	-2%	90%
Chemistry	-12%	-2%	10%
Physics	-128%	-13%	115%
Social Studies 30-1	-17%	27%	44%
Social Studies 30-2	-42%	17%	59%

June results (see table 6.4) demonstrate how females were *failed* less frequently by their teachers in every subject; however, females were failed at a higher percentage on five of the *standardized provincial examinations that were marked anonymously*. When class marks and provincial tests are viewed side by side, the third column demonstrates how much more females are advantaged, due to the large discrepancies between the two types of assessments. High levels of grade inflation evident in class assessments by teachers, *who are not marking students' exams anonymously*, compensate for females' lower achievement on provincial standardized tests.

Notably, on Social Studies 30-1, females were failed in their class marks less frequently than males by 30 percent; however, on the provincial diploma examinations, females failed 31 percent more frequently, which placed them

Table 6.4 June 2016: Not Achieving the Acceptable Standard (Did *not* meet and therefore must retake the course)(Example: In ELA 30-2, 36 percent more males were assessed as "failed" from their teacher. In the provincial exam, 12 percent more males failed. The female advantage from the school mark is that 24 percent fewer girls failed.)

Subject	School Mark	Diploma Exam	Female Advantage
ELA 30-2	-36%	-12%	24%
ELA 30-1	-43%	-4%	39%
Math 30-1	-48%	2%	50%
Math 30-2	-55%	-30%	25%
Biology	-6%	3%	9%
Science	-62%	-1%	61%
Chemistry	-20%	12%	32%
Physics	-124%	-6%	118%
Social Studies 30-1	-30%	31%	-1%
Social Studies 30-2	-57%	11%	68%

at an overall disadvantage by 1 percent. In Physics, females' classroom failure rates were 124 percent less than the rate for males; in contrast, females failed the diploma examinations more frequently (6 percent), but they still were advantaged by 118 percent less failures when the two sets of marks were combined.

It is also noteworthy that on the twenty examinations conducted during these two semesters, only on two occasions—for example, the ELA 30-1 exam, at -5 percent (table 6.1), and the Math 30-2 exam, at -16 (table 6.2) percent—were females disadvantaged when comparing Standard of Excellence class marks with the provincial examination marks. Females were disadvantaged in only one subject (the Social Studies 30-1 exam at -1 percent [table 6.4]) when a similar comparison combining marks for meeting the Acceptable Standard was conducted.

In the runup to the provincial election in 2015, the Alberta government sought to pander for the teachers' union support by altering the weight of the two components that led to students' final marks. The standard for many decades had been to weight the class marks equally with the provincial diploma exam (50/50). Beginning in 2016, however, the Alberta government implemented a new weighting standard, with class marks accounting for 70 percent, thus making this component more than twice the value of the provincial tests, which were professionally prepared, extensively field-tested, and marked anonymously.

Table 6.5 provides an example of how this new formula (70/30) further exaggerates the advantage females have enjoyed, as was demonstrated in table 6.1 (January 2016: Standard of Excellence—equivalent to an A).

This revised, blended grading system instituted by the Alberta government is highly misleading, particularly when the school-awarded marks and the diploma examination marks diverge. A confidential e-mail from a provincial examination manager revealed a situation in a school in which there was a

Table 6.5   January 2016: Standard of Excellence (Equivalent to an A) with Impact of 70/30 Weighting in Favor of Class Mark Indicated in Brackets and Bold Print

Subject	School Mark	Diploma Exam	Female Advantage
ELA 30-2	67% **(154%)**	26%	41% **(128%)**
ELA 30-1	48% **(110%)**	53%	-5% **(57%)**
Math 30-1	8% **(23%)**	-5%	13% **(23%)**
Math 30-2	59% **(136%)**	50%	9% **(86%)**
Biology	5% **(12%)**	-4%	9% **(16%)**
Science	31% **(71%)**	27%	4% **(44%)**
Chemistry	2% **(5%)**	-7%	9% **(12%)**
Physics	13% **(30%)**	1%	12% **(31%)**
Social Studies 30-1	19% **(44%)**	-14%	33% **(58%)**
Social Studies 30-2	33% **(76%)**	-1%	34% **(75%)**

class averaging over 80% on the school-awarded mark and less than 50% on the Diploma Examination mark. The resulting blended average, a grade likely in the low 70% range (under the new 70/30 blend), is not the result of any assessment evidence justifying this grade, yet this grade could be used to determine a student's post-secondary eligibility.

Grade inflation occurring in classrooms, further inflated by a factor of 2.3 in the 70/30 newly adopted weighting regimen, clearly identifies which gender—i.e., females—will win future awards, scholarships, and placements in university programs.

As an example, Alberta has two major universities—in Edmonton and in Calgary—and their undergraduate enrollment already reports a decided advantage for female students. In U of A (Edmonton), for example, there were 12,962 males and 16,138 females registered in their most recent public report (2011), providing females with 55.5 percent of their university placements. In Calgary, their 2015 report provided placements for 10,667 males and 12,146 females, resulting in 53.3 percent of their university placements for female students. *In addition, the female-advantaged ratio will increase substantially with the government's decision to weight class marks higher, by a factor of 2.3:1.*

GRADE INFLATION'S GENDER ADVANTAGE

The foregoing documentation provides evidence of the female-gender advantage in British Columbia and Alberta, two of the high-achieving school systems according to the PISA 2015 assessments of fifteen-year-old students. The problem of grade inflation continually begs the question: Does every student have an inflated mark, or do only some students? Unfairness occurs when different criteria are used when students' work is assessed.

The Fraser Institute (FI) in Canada routinely posts reviews on its website for provincial test results that demonstrate gender differences in *elementary-school* grades in three provinces: British Columbia, Alberta, and Ontario. The FI also posts reviews of Quebec's *secondary-school* results. These reviews for the 2014–2015 school year compare percentages of schools across the respective provinces in which one gender's achievement in language arts (reading) and mathematics was higher:

- Ontario (Grade 6):
    The reading gender gap favored females at 71.7 percent of schools, males at 13.8 percent of schools, and the count was even at 14.5 percent of schools. The math gender gap favored females at 45.6 percent of schools,

males at 40.5 percent of schools, and the count was even at 13.9 percent of schools.

- British Columbia (Grade 7):

    The reading gender gap favored females at 62.7 percent of schools, males at 36.7 percent of schools, and the count was even at 0.6 percent of schools. The math gender gap favored females at 36.7 percent of schools, males at 62.1 percent of schools, and the count was even at 1.2 percent of schools.

- Alberta (Grade 6):

    The language arts gender gap favored females at 88.8 percent of schools, males at 10.9 percent of schools, and the count was even at 0.3 percent of schools. The math gender gap favored males at 49.4 percent of schools, females at 49.7 percent of schools, and the count was even at 0.9 percent of schools.

- Quebec (Secondary):

    In language instruction, females scored higher in 95 percent of the schools, while males scored the highest in 72 percent of the schools in mathematics.

These comparisons, reflecting percentages of schools rather than percentages of students, *overwhelmingly favor female results on reading standardized tests.* Chapter 3 of this book provides a partial explanation for these results, based on research that indicates the advantage female students enjoy from learning in classrooms dominated by female teachers. The head start that female students gain from these early years under the instruction of female teachers remains throughout the years until their graduation; however, the paucity of male teachers in the primary grades makes it virtually impossible to assess the impact of gender instruction on male students.

In mathematics, the percentages of schools in which male students scored higher levels of achievement on system tests were substantially different in British Columbia and Quebec. In tables 6.2 to 6.5, which compared marks for Mathematics 30-1 (the upper-stream course), males scored marginally higher than females on the diploma exams, while females received higher results from their classroom teachers. The advantage for females was 13 percent in the January testing and 8 percent in the June testing. A record of classroom marks for a comparison with these test results was not provided by FI.

In addition to the analysis of gender-based learning undertaken by the FI, Voyer (2014) provided a *meta-analysis* from 308 studies reflecting the grades of 538,710 boys and 595,332 girls. Seventy percent of the samples were comprised of students from the United States, with the remainder coming from more than thirty other countries. Voyer's conclusions are as follows:

Although gender differences follow essentially stereotypical patterns on achievement tests in which boys typically score higher on math and science, females have the advantage on school grades regardless of the material. School marks reflect learning in the larger social context of the classroom and require effort and persistence over long periods of time, whereas standardized tests assess basic or specialized academic abilities and aptitudes at one point in time without social influences.

Based on research from 1914 through 2011 that spanned more than 30 countries, the study found the differences in grades between girls and boys were largest for language courses and smallest for math and science. The female advantage in school performance in math and science did not become apparent until junior or middle school. The degree of gender difference in grades increased from elementary to middle school, but decreased between high school and college.

The study reveals that recent claims of a "boy crisis," with boys lagging behind girls in school achievement, are not accurate, because girls' grades have been *consistently higher than boys'* across several decades with no significant changes in recent years.

The fact that females generally perform better than their male counterparts throughout what is essentially mandatory schooling in most countries seems to be a well-kept secret, considering how little attention it has received as a global phenomenon.

As for why girls perform better in school than boys, Voyer speculated *that social and cultural factors could be among several possible explanations. Parents may assume boys are better at math and science* so they might encourage girls to put more effort into their studies, which could lead to the slight advantage girls have in all courses. Gender differences in learning styles is another possibility. Previous research has shown girls tend to study in order to understand the materials, whereas boys emphasize performance, which indicates a focus on the final grades. Mastery of the subject matter generally produces better marks than performance emphasis, so this could account in part for males' lower marks than females.

Voyer's analysis is important, because the results are based on findings from many different cultures in addition to the predominantly American students. The conclusions that females perennially—actually, for many decades—have received *higher marks from classroom teachers*, and that these differences are greatest in the language arts, are consistent with the conclusions presented in this book. Therefore, a new and current "boy crisis" based on student academic achievement is not the primary issue, because this phenomenon is not a recent one.

A similar conclusion is evident in the statement speculating that "social and cultural factors could be among several possible explanations." Herein is the issue that is the specific purpose for this book. Incorporating social and cultural factors in students' classroom grading opens the door to *subjectivity* when assessing academic achievement. In other words, teacher bias is introduced when these factors become a significant part of the assessment process, and the central message of this book is that *assessments of learning should not be conflated with behavior or cultural issues.*

Douglas Reeves, an American expert on assessment, provided an insightful exchange of e-mails when he stated that the "teacher bias that I have observed is most insidious not in the tests themselves, but in the conflation of academic performance and behavior when translating test performance into marks for the report card." If student behavior influences the letter grades assigned by teachers, are there some students whose behavior advantages them more than others?

If there is a discernible pattern that demonstrates such a bias, then the issue of fairness rears its ugly head. Reeves explains that

> students (disproportionately minority girls in my research) receive higher letter grades for lower actual achievement, because of their quiet, compliant and respectful attitude. I will note, parenthetically, that I'm all in favor of quiet, compliant and respectful behavior among teenagers—I just wish that we would not call these characteristics "algebra" or "physics."

Webber et al. (2009) similarly concluded that culture influenced student marks, stating that "almost 60 percent of educators perceived that students' cultural background affected the grades these students got."

Reeves explains further how this bias serves to *disadvantage male students*, and adds the observation that teachers readily discern a dichotomy between test and class marks:

> Other students (disproportionately boys) receive lower letter grades for higher actual achievement, because of disorganization and oppositional behavior. Every time I ask teachers if they can think of students who make As and Bs on tests yet receive Ds or Fs in the class, almost every hand goes up.

Harlen (2004), synthesizing twenty-three studies from the United Kingdom and the United States, also concluded that evidence of gender bias exists, stating that "teachers' judgments of the academic performance of young children are influenced by the teachers' assessment of their behavior; this adversely affects the assessment of boys compared with girls." Scantlebury (2009) stated it somewhat differently: "Overall, teachers have *lower expectations* for girls' academic success compared to boys."

Webber et al., after surveying and interviewing teachers, found that a surprisingly high percentage acknowledged a *gender bias*:

Almost 1 in 4 (23%) of educators agree "students' gender" affects the grades they get. However, qualitative data suggests that frequently gender was linked with behavior in that boys were perceived to be more likely to be disruptive and less compliant, which in turn influenced the grades that teachers assigned to boys.

In other words, while only one in four teachers *openly* acknowledged gender bias, the interview process revealed the potential for boys to be disadvantaged when having their work assessed because of their *lower levels of compliant behavior.*

It is discouraging to think that biases based on gender could find their way into our school systems. We expect fairness and consistency to be foundational in our society; yet *we don't expect it to occur in our classrooms.* Some stakeholders may feel defensive about this unacceptable situation, and so the regional study delved into this issue at considerable length by assessing gender bias for students from grades 1 through to university placement.

In our region's mathematics tests, male students scored higher on grades 3, 6, and 9 system tests at both the Acceptable Standard and the Standard of Excellence levels. However, when teachers were required to complete student report cards and provide a *classroom assessment* of student achievement in grades 1 through 9, more males were assessed as functioning *below their grade level—in every grade.* In these evaluations, students' final marks were based exclusively on the teachers' assessments without their knowing how the students had performed on the standardized tests, because the system tests were given in the final week of the school year, after the report cards with the teachers' assessments had already been completed.

At the end of grade 9, each student had the opportunity to *self-select* a mathematics stream for senior high school that would lead to university programming. Unfortunately for male students, the programming decisions were made in April for the following September, but because system tests occurred at the end of June, *their classroom marks weighed heavily in the decisions.* Students and their parents did not receive their grade-9 *system* test results until the end of September, well after they had already begun their grade-10 courses. Thus, participation rates in the grade-10, *upper-stream mathematics courses* favored females, even though males demonstrated higher proficiency on the system tests taken at the end of June (too late to be considered in the decision-making process).

This aspect of the study is significant, because grade-10 programming is the first screen for students' ability to choose a career path. Enrolling in the lower-stream mathematics course ultimately curtails qualification for university acceptance, and consequently a student's career aspirations. Mathematics is a significant *gatekeeper course into the world of work,* and the current screening process, influenced by the biases presented here, is eliminating many males from contending.

With this disadvantage in *gaining placement* in upper-stream mathematics courses, male students continue to experience a negative bias that further limits their potential for scholarships and acceptance into universities. In this study, school-awarded marks and examination marks each counted for 50 percent of final course marks, and more female students received the Standard of Excellence from the *school-awarded marks*, while more males received this high standard on their diploma examinations. *This pattern of assessment was consistent over a period of seven consecutive semesters.*

From the broader perspective of examining all courses in English, mathematics, the sciences, and social studies, the analysis underscores a consistent advantage for female students. *Aggregating seven consecutive semesters* across these courses—seventy tests—females received *almost double* the A marks received by males from teachers' *class marks*—i.e., 13.3 percent of females received As, while 6.7 percent of males received As. *Diploma examination marks*, however, told a different story, as male students scoring A marks averaged 8.7 percent, while female students scoring As averaged 9.0 percent. When combining and weighing both sets of marks equally, females held a substantial advantage—gleaned from their higher set of classroom marks.

When considering only the *upper-stream courses*, which are the critical determinants for accessing placement in universities, school-level A marks were 66 percent more frequently awarded than A marks in diploma examination, thus demonstrating the high level of grade inflation in these important subjects. *Classroom-level* A marks favored females by 11.4 percent, while *examination* A marks favored males by 8.1 percent. Because the data set demonstrates significant grade inflation at the school level, females have received a substantial advantage in securing scholarships and placement into the more prestigious universities.

One superintendent who became aware of these disturbing trends undertook a study in his own school district. He tracked all student marks by gender as each progressed through high school, and he monitored the trends as students moved from one teacher gender to another. His review revealed several troubling discoveries: Female students moving from a grade in which their teacher was a female to a grade in which their teacher was a male experienced a *bump up* in their marks. While males progressing from a male teacher to a female teacher also benefited, the bump up was not considered significant.

When the superintendent informed the principals in his school district of these findings, he was greatly disturbed by their responses. They *readily acknowledged* the situation, referring to it as the "halter-top effect." This sad revelation underscores how teacher bias can obviate efforts to ensure fairness for students.

The advantage for female students evident in the regional study also translated into a 2007 StatCan national report for Canada titled "Why Are Most University Students Women?" A review of this study states that

> the gap in university attendance is largely associated with differences in academic performance and study habits at the age of 15, parental expectations, and other characteristics of men and women.... Weaker academic performance among men accounted for almost one half (45%) of the gap. Specifically, young men had lower overall school marks at age 15 and had poorer performance on a standardized reading test. (see http://www.statcan.gc.ca/daily-quotidien/070920/dq070920b-eng.htm)

Within the report itself, the authors explain:

> In the 2001 Census, universities had clearly become the domain of women, as they made up 58 percent of all graduates.... We find the differences in the characteristics of boys and girls account for more than three quarters (76.8%) of the gap in university participation. In order of importance, the main factors are differences in school marks at age 15 (31.8%), standardized test scores in reading at age 15 (14.6%), study habits (11.1%), parental expectations (8.5%) and the university earnings premium relative to high school (5.3%). (Frenette and Zeman 2007)

The *school mark* is the primary answer to the question, "Why are most university students women?" The message in this study is made more significant when it is understood that most Canadian students progressing from high school to a university submit marks *only generated by their teachers*. In other words, most provinces do not have exit examinations in grade 12 that counterbalance the more biased marks from teachers. The "weaker academic performance among men" is a significant factor here, given the evidence that demonstrates *their marks have been impacted negatively by the men's noncompliant behavior.*

When the school system does not implement *standardized testing with anonymous marking,* the male students become disadvantaged when seeking entry into universities. York University in Ontario already is reporting their enrollment as being 70 percent female. This is significant because the province of Ontario suffers from the highest levels of grade inflation in Canada. *And the higher the rate of grade inflation, the greater the potential for female acceptance into universities, because of their more compliant school behavior.*

This disadvantage is corroborated in the United States by another study released in an October 2006 article, "Learning and Gender," published in the *American School Board Journal.* In it, the authors suggested what administrators might find when examining their districts:

Boys, they'll probably notice, make up 80 to 90 percent of the district's discipline referrals, 70 percent of learning disabled children, and at least two-thirds of the children on behavioral medication. They'll probably find that boys earn two-thirds of the Ds and Fs in the district, but less than half [of] the As.

In the author's regional study, three times as many male students were coded with "moderate" or "severe" disabilities, and two times more with "mild" or "moderate" disabilities. At the same time, males who were coded with different types of disabilities generally *tended to outperform* coded females when teachers assessed their grade level of achievement. In other words, *more male students were identified as "special needs," but they were assessed as demonstrating higher achievement by their teachers.* An obvious question is whether all of these males should have been coded in the first place, or were they simply "being boys" in a female-dominated world? Definitely, *concern about fairness for boys and girls specifically is a transformational issue for education.*

One message to this point that is emphasized in the book is that *grade inflation resulting from low standards or low expectations that teachers have of their students is a significant problem in our education systems.* Students and their parents receive false information about how well the academic curriculum has been learned. This misleading information instills a *false sense of security* in students, who then lose motivation to contribute their best efforts. And ultimately, taxpayers are robbed of students who have been sufficiently prepared to maximize their potential later in society.

A second message follows the first, but it should increase our trepidation concerning the effectiveness of our school systems. *Grade inflation is not equally applied across all students; rather, it favors the female gender with an advantage in securing awards, scholarships, and placement in prestigious university programs.* This disadvantage toward males may be unfair, but it is frequently disregarded and kept hidden from public scrutiny, because educators do not want to lose the confidence of the taxpayers and their government representatives.

For teachers and their unions, the resolution of this unfairness involves an unpalatable acquiescence to the use of standardized testing, in which a teacher's individual control over the construction of the assessment is lost and students' anonymity is ensured. Perhaps of even greater importance here is that any use of standardized testing achieves a higher level of accountability in the results, and such increased transparency in system quality not only has implications for the educators in the school system, but also for the politicians who are ultimately responsible for that system.

THE KEY POINTS MADE IN THIS CHAPTER ARE:

- British Columbia and Alberta, both high-performing provinces on the PISA assessments, are plagued with high levels of grade inflation in classroom marks when compared with diploma examinations, which favor female students.
- Several Canadian provinces demonstrate grade inflation at the classroom level, favoring female students in middle-school grades.
- A meta-analysis of research concludes that females perennially—actually, for many decades—have received *higher marks from classroom teachers*, and that these differences are greatest in the subject of language arts.
- The meta-analysis also concludes that *social and cultural factors* play a role in females' receiving higher classroom marks. This is unacceptable.
- Bias against male students is a worldwide phenomenon.

Chapter 7

The Males' Ship Is Listing Badly

Inconsistent marking by classroom teachers of their students' work is a significant problem, with *assessments generally skewed upward*, thus creating a condition referred to as *grade inflation*. Equally problematic is the propensity for teachers to allow biases, most notably in favor of students' compliant behavior, to influence their marking, which advantages female students when school systems dispense awards and scholarships. Marks are also a student's currency for gaining entry into prestigious university programs, and the *grade-inflation advantage enjoyed by female students ensures that more of them are successful with their applications.*

The politically correct response, if the situation was reversed, would produce strong criticisms that the situation is unfair—which it would be. Millennia of historically documented male domination of females justifies continuing efforts at ensuring equal opportunities and rights for females, and these have definitely occurred. However, *the issue currently requiring attention in our education system is whether assessments of learning should be conflated with social and cultural factors such as compliant behavior, neatness of work, minority status, etc.*

Permitting these types of biases to influence assessments of learning, which our evidence corroborates, disadvantages male students in the schools' female-dominated workplace and is unfair. Other strategies have historically been implemented, such as affirmative action where formulae are transparently utilized, and these do, in fact, adjust a legitimate cultural need. However, the current injustice is penalizing male students unfairly—with lifelong consequences—and it is a reverse discrimination requiring an immediate public debate. But such thoughtful discussion cannot occur *until the matter is exposed for public scrutiny*, which is the purpose of this book.

71

POSTSECONDARY BLOCKAGE

A key concern occurs when students graduate from high school and endeavor to pursue their career interests. We have already indicated that some males are inappropriately culled by inflated assessments favoring females when schools introduce streaming for high-school courses. Ongoing unfair assessments through high-school programs further damage males' successful applications for postsecondary opportunities, which has a negative impact on male students' achieving fulfilling career choices and potential earnings later in life. In other words, many male students are unfairly penalized in elementary and high school, which perpetuates lifelong injustices.

Mounting evidence demonstrates the extent to which unfairness is now at least several decades old. In Canada, for example, a StatCan report in 2013–2014 chronicles this trend, as well as a partial assessment of why it is occurring:

> Women have progressed considerably in terms of education and schooling over the past few decades. Just 20 years ago, a smaller percentage of women than men aged 25 to 54 had a postsecondary education. Today, the situation is completely different. Education indicators show that women generally do better than men. This gap in favour of women is even noticeable at a young age, since girls often get better marks than boys in elementary and secondary school. (Turcotte 2011)

This report affirms the core message of this book regarding which gender receives higher marks from their classroom teachers. This analysis, however, does not delve into the next step and compare classroom marks with standardized assessments utilizing anonymous marking—which is the critical analysis necessary for understanding the current gender bias. Figure 7.1 portrays how this unchecked grade inflation in Canada's classrooms ultimately translated into a gender advantage for females *in every province by the year 2009.*

A noteworthy demographic demonstrated in figure 7.1 is the relative parity evident in Alberta, the bastion of standardized testing in Canada. Despite claims that the province's oil patch lures many males away from postsecondary institutions, Alberta offers the greatest parity in citizens holding a degree. This province has a history of recording the lowest levels of grade inflation across the nation, an outcome attributed to the use of standardized assessments in grades 3, 6, 9, and 12. *These assessments serve as a check and balance in the school system, so that educators know whether they are allowing classroom standards to creep downward, resulting in grade inflation.*

On the other hand, two different provinces—Saskatchewan and Prince Edward Island—did not use any form of provincial testing, and the disparity

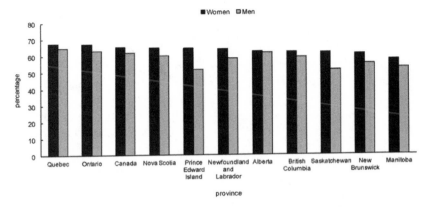

Figure 7.1   Percentage of Women and Men with a Postsecondary Education, by Province, 2009 (www.statcan.gc.ca/pub/89-503-x/2010001/article/11542/c-g/c-g002-eng.htm)

between male and female degree holders is greater than 10 percent, *more than double the percentages of all other provinces.* These two provinces have a history of students receiving high class marks from their teachers while faring less well on national and international assessments. The gender disparity evident in figure 7.1 provides credence to our concern regarding female students benefiting with higher marks from classroom teachers.

Pratt (2011) provides additional insight into this phenomenon in an interview with Dan Seneker, the manager of undergraduate recruitment at the University of Saskatchewan in Saskatoon, regarding his views on provincial diploma examinations:

> He has heard over the years from lots of Alberta parents concerned that their kids are at a disadvantage in competing for spots in top faculties and for scholarship money because they are held to a higher standard with the diploma exams. The exams so often pull down a student's marks that Alberta students are less likely to graduate with an A average. Of course, there are always kids who do brilliantly on exams and good for them. In lots of cases, the exams—that no other students in the country have to write—work to lower a mark of lots of smart kids even by a few points and that can make an enormous difference— whether you get into medical school or engineering.

These words from a recruitment manager are consistent with the messages set forth in this book related to grade inflation. Diploma examinations are actually *presented as a culprit* in holding Alberta graduates from gaining entry into universities; yet the examination questions are prepared annually by teams of teachers from across the province under the supervision of a full-time manager; are thoroughly vetted through field testing in classrooms of students to reduce both bias and confusion; and are marked by at least two teachers, with the writers' identity kept anonymous.

One nugget for understanding the grade inflation problem is evident in the recruitment manager's words that "he has heard over the years from lots of Alberta parents concerned that their kids are at a disadvantage in competing for spots in top faculties and for scholarship money because they are held to a higher standard with the diploma exams." *Simply put, if marks are getting so low within an organization, such as a school, a school district, or a province, that they affect students' entry into a university, the organization should resolve the issue by lowering standards.* An organization's students will be more likely to win if it inflates students' grades. And if it goes undetected, such fraudulent activity typically works. Inflating students' grades is not legally punished—at least not yet.

The province of Ontario provides an example of how its educational system responded to the issue of limited spaces in universities. According to a "Making the Grade" report in the *Queen's Journal* on September 19, 2008, 90 percent of Ontario's students had a B average or greater, and 60 percent of students applying to a university had an A average. In other words, teachers were making certain that their students would get the chance to qualify despite the shortage of university seats; the reporter concluded that "the number of A-students isn't growing because people are getting smarter. Rather, academic standards have declined so [that] it is easier to get an A than ever before—a phenomenon known as grade inflation" (Woods 2008).

Forgotten in this analysis is the fact that grade inflation is not occurring equally across the spectrum of students. Winners and losers exist *because classroom assessments lack the quality of system examinations*, thereby allowing bias to creep into the process and result in unfairness. Males are the most prevalent victims in the flawed process of relying exclusively on classroom assessments, and *governments that choose to ignore the outcomes become the villains in their unfair treatment of male students.*

Pratt's article goes on to say that "Alberta can be proud that it holds students to a higher standard. Students here are marked harder, and those that manage to go on to post-secondary do better—that is, their marks don't drop as much at university, Seneker found." In other words, Alberta's students' achievement is more closely aligned with the expectations of Saskatchewan universities' expectations for students who enter their programs, which should be the true basis upon which university placement selections should be determined.

An attempt to understand the relatively recent turnabout in gender acceptance into universities, as documented in figure 7.1, is what motivated Karas (2011) to examine the issue of male students being assessed by a female teacher:

At UVic [University of Victoria, British Columbia], 57.1 percent of current undergraduate students are female and 42.9 percent are male, according to Tony Eder, a director for UVic's Institutional Planning and Analysis.... This trend is escalated by an increasing number of males dropping out of PSIs [postsecondary institutions] worldwide. Eder explains that the exact number is difficult to track because there is no way of concluding whether it is [due to] a leave of absence or a more permanent decision....

Jamie Cassels, UVic's Vice-President Academic and Provost, believes there's not yet an answer for this phenomenon: "For almost 10 years, it's been like that: a female population that is at about 60 percent versus 40 percent for males. And it varies. It's interesting that it's not getting worse. The question for me is, is it even a problem? If it is a problem, are there barriers and problems at the university level, or is it happening somewhere else?"

One theory suggests [that] the gap between males and females begins in elementary school due to the fact that the vast majority of elementary teachers are female, and the mentoring position teachers have at such a young age.... Teaching is female-oriented and that means a lot of boys don't have role models in the education system. They lose motivation to go further.

Karis's conclusion provides only one theory to explain the gender gap in the universities, and the theory that the paucity of male role models in our school system is the cause is consistent with the explanations given in this book.

Drolet (2007) examined this problem of the gender gap and proffered his perspective: The gender gap is a fact in most OECD countries, but he wonders whether this is just an interesting sociological phenomenon, or a symptom of some deeper problem for males. He ultimately concludes that no one is quite sure, referencing an American researcher, Rob Crosnoe, a social psychologist at the University of Texas at Austin, who observes a concern also consistent with this book's themes:

But there's a conundrum: while girls are getting better grades overall in math and science classes, boys are doing better on standardized tests. People are still trying to figure out what's going on there. It could mean that the grades that girls are getting in math and science reflect lots of different things, like behaviour and effort and things that aren't reflected in a standardized test.

Conflating behavior with learning for deriving final marks of academic achievement is a critical issue. When a student is being assessed on the ability to multiply fractions or understand meanings from a paragraph, should the student's mark be influenced by his or her classroom behavior? One senior administrator contributed his personal feelings of bias when conducting assessments of students' work when he was a classroom teacher. His explanation of the insidious nature of bias was evident when he described the differences in marking work submitted by students whose parents were, respectively, the city's mayor, the police chief, the town drunk, a cousin of the teacher, a neighbor of the teacher, etc.

His examples demonstrate the importance of *anonymous marking*, and how this contributes to fairness. Seldom do teachers ensure that assignments are marked completely anonymously, and, indeed, even less often does a teacher in one school exchange assignments with one from another school in order to ensure total anonymity. During their conferences, parents should request that this strategy be employed.

THE PUBLIC'S FOCUS ON GENDER IMBALANCE

Fortunately, media attention regarding gender imbalance in postsecondary institutions is increasing, and *Macleans* magazine (August 12, 2013) published a list of Canadian universities with more than 66 percent female students:

1. Mount Saint Vincent University, Halifax: 75 percent
2. NSCAD University, Halifax: 74 percent
3. Université du Québec en Outaouais, Gatineau, Quebec: 71 percent
4. Alberta College of Art + Design, Calgary: 70 percent
5. Université du Québec à Rimouski, Rimouski, Quebec: 70 percent
6. Université Sainte-Anne, Church Point, Nova Scotia: 70 percent
7. Emily Carr University of Art + Design, Vancouver: 69 percent
8. OCAD University, Toronto: 69 percent
9. Brandon University, Brandon, Manitoba: 68 percent
10. Nipissing University, North Bay, Ontario: 68 percent
11. Saint Thomas University, Fredericton, New Brunswick: 68 percent

Macleans did identify one institution—the Royal Military College of Canada, Kingston, Ontario—with more than two-thirds male enrollment, at 82 percent.

The U.S. media have also become more attentive to the shifting gender enrollment in colleges and universities. Rocheleau (2016) reports that women accounted for 55 percent of undergraduates enrolled at four-year colleges in the United States as of the fall of 2014. *His report concluded that this gender gap would continue to grow in the coming years*, according to some projections, and that some experts say, "The higher incidence of behavioral and school disciplinary problems among boys may be a factor." This statement about behavior is wide open to interpretation, but it is the crux of the matter in this book.

Pew Research Center researchers Lopez and Gonzalez-Barrera (2014) examine the trend of high-school graduates who enrolled in college in 1994 and in 2012.

- Among Hispanics, males enrolled in college increased from 52 to 62 percent, but female enrollment increased from 52 to 76 percent: *a female-over-male net increase of 14 percent.*
- Among Blacks, male enrollment increased from 56 to 57 percent, but female enrollment increased from 48 to 69 percent: *a female-over-male net increase of 20 percent.*
- Among Whites, male enrollment remained the same at 62 percent, but female enrollment increased from 66 to 72 percent: *a female-over-male net increase of 6 percent.*
- Among Asians, males enrolled in college increased from 82 to 83 percent, but female enrollment increased from 81 to 86 percent: *a female-over-male net increase of 4 percent.*

In each of these four groupings, the percentage of females enrolling outstripped the males. The phenomenon of females enrolling in postsecondary educational institutions at greater rates than males is also a concern in the United Kingdom. Ratcliffe (2013) reported that in 2010–2011, there were more female (55 percent) than male (45 percent) full-time undergraduates enrolled in a university—a trend that, he suggested, showed no sign of ending.

Similarly, Australia has reported that the gender gap among their domestic students has widened to almost 20 percent—up from 16.2 percent a decade ago—and Martin (2015) reports that a leading education expert is calling for the lack of men at university to be considered an equity issue. Martin quotes this education expert as claiming, "The imbalance began in school years. We have got a national issue to face up to, and that is particularly in middle and secondary [schooling]. Young men are not doing as well as they should."

This pattern of females being the dominant group in postsecondary education is consistent across Europe, with one exception: According to Eurostat's report of 2013, more than 19.6 million students were in attendance at universities across the continent, comprised of approximately 9 million males and 10.7 million females. Out of the thirty-four countries in Europe, only Germany reported a majority of male students.

There is not a right or wrong answer regarding gender participation in postsecondary education, but a significant cultural shift toward female participation is increasingly evident. Factors bringing about this shift are complex and difficult to calculate, but it is impossible to ignore the amount of research that demonstrates the impact of males being taught almost exclusively by female teachers in the early grades, and the biases teachers bring to the assessment of student learning.

There is no equivocation that ignoring this shift is as unfair as are many biases existing against females. However, even in our modern societies, school systems in which male children are stifled from achieving their potential are not in any society's best interest. The next chapter's focus is on the workplace, where the consequences of these gender biases truly become evident.

THE KEY POINTS MADE IN THIS CHAPTER ARE:

- Marks are a student's currency for gaining entry into university programs, *and the grade inflation advantage enjoyed by female students ensures that more females are successful with their applications.*
- Some males are inappropriately culled by inflated assessments favoring females when schools introduce a policy of streaming for high-school courses.
- Unchecked grade inflation in Canada's classrooms had translated into a significant gender advantage for females in every province by 2009.
- Males are the usual victims in the flawed process of relying exclusively on classroom assessments.
- The gender gap in education is a proven fact in most OECD countries.
- Media attention regarding gender imbalance in postsecondary institutions is increasing.

Chapter 8

Males: The Hidden Underclass

Calculating the long-term effects of gender bias in education within our culture is fraught with both challenge and risk, because the multiplicity of decisions that people make throughout their days, years, and lifetimes make understanding the cause and effect of this issue very complex. This book is about one pervasive issue that occurs over many years while students are within the K-12 school system, and that is particularly focused on the disadvantage that one gender (the male gender) experiences while proceeding through to high-school graduation and university placement.

Males begin their school careers in the elementary grades with almost exclusively female teachers, who teach from a perspective not entirely consistent with the learning styles of their male students. Learning to read is the major emphasis in primary-school education, and *the absence of male teacher role models during this critical stage results in a period of time when male students gradually fall behind their female peers.* Male students' lack of success during this crucial time is a deterrent to the development of a healthy concept of their ability to learn and be successful in school—and in life.

Compounding this concern about the absence of gender role models during this early stage of development is the ongoing problem in schools regarding low standards in classrooms, which ultimately produce unacceptable levels of grade inflation. This problem would not be so egregious if the impact of grade inflation were equally applied to all students, but it is not. The research demonstrates a consistent pattern of bias *disadvantaging male students because of behavior that can be generally described as noncompliant.*

This unfairness, which penalizes students by *conflating* their progress in learning with their behavior, disqualifies some males when they seek to progress into the high-school courses necessary for successful university placement. Too many males are unfairly eliminated from obtaining awards, scholarships, and acceptance into prestigious university programs *that could energize their commitment for achieving their potential.* This concern became especially evident as society entered the Information Age. Fewer career paths now remain from the Industrial Age, which, in past years, provided employment for many males who might have been disqualified from pursuing higher ambitions.

The unfortunate outcome of how schools have failed our male students is now evident. Governments frequently pursue the popular mandate of "jobs, jobs, jobs," because unemployment creates an unhealthy economic system that detracts from an unemployed individual's self-worth. Therefore, monitoring data such as unemployment rates is a popular activity among politicians and the media. However, unemployment statistics have lost their value in recent years, because workers who have completely withdrawn themselves from the workforce are not tabulated into unemployment rates, as these figures only consider those persons who are actively seeking employment.

On its website, the OECD demonstrates how significant the problem has become in several nations, but especially in North America. A significant number of men between the ages of twenty-five and fifty-four withdrew from the labor force between 1990 and 2009. While the male participation rate in Japan only dropped from approximately 97.5 percent to 96 percent, Canada declined from 93 percent to 91 percent, and the United States dropped from 93.3 percent to 90 percent.

Narrowing the focus to youth unemployment—of persons under twenty-five years of age—provides an even more revealing description. In Canada, in 2014, male unemployment in this age group was 14.8 percent, which was 2.8 percent higher than that of females. The disparity was even greater in 2015, when the unemployment rate of males in this age group was 15.1 percent, compared with female unemployment at 10.9 percent. For 2016, 14.3 percent of males in this age group were unemployed, compared with 11.5 percent of females. In the United States, in 2014, the unemployment rate of males in this age group was at 15.3 percent, whereas female unemployment was at only 10.7 percent.

In a problem as complex as the male dropout rate from a nation's workforce, *one factor on the list of causes* that must be considered is that too many males were excluded from pursuing their potential by a school system that conflated their behavior with their academic achievement. Too many male high-school students are deprived of entry into college and university programs because the school's marker bias has contributed to a set of flawed marks, thus deflating their success rates. A change in the process is required that will ensure fair assessment of *all* students' work, so that entry selection into postsecondary programs is truly based on merit.

The general lack of awareness regarding the school systems' contribution to male unemployment rates merely exacerbates the problem. Herein is the root of the dilemma: Schools provide the initial training for the nation's workforce, and when the issue of gender bias is not acknowledged and explored at this level, it impedes any remedy for concerns identified later in life. Our education systems play a significant role in permitting unfair biases in classrooms to sideline an inordinate percentage of the male student population—and it affects them throughout their lifetimes.

The *LA Times* attempted to scratch the veneer of this problem in an article written by Jim Puzzanghera, published on November 21, 2016. He stated, "Economists said increased globalization and the decline in factory jobs has played a major role in pushing prime-aged men, particularly those with less education, out of the workforce." The *lack of sufficient education* is the link here, however, with the message in this chapter being that too many males are *derailed from pursuing higher levels of education.*

The *LA Times* article went on to explain that 14 percent of the absentee workers were enrolled in courses to upgrade their qualifications, and this undoubtedly included a portion of those affected by their earlier school systems' biases. Undoubtedly, some of these males had been deprived of their fair opportunities when attending school and they now had to play catchup.

The Barberbiz website, accessed on November 6, 2016, provided more detail regarding the "Missing Men" in the United States, stating that "83 percent of men in the prime working ages of 25–54 who were not in the labor force had not worked in the previous year." Barber pointed out a critical issue:

> Men now account for only 42 percent of college graduates, meaning that men in the current generation will be enormously underrepresented in the well-paying professions that require a college degree. Former Treasury Secretary Lawrence H. Summers, now professor of economics at Harvard, estimates that a third of men between 24 and 54 without college educations could be out of work by mid-century.

Again, a frustration is expressed regarding the lack of males in college, but there is *limited explanation regarding the problem's root cause.* These well-intentioned "experts" are focused more on factors at play when males have already become adults, than what might have occurred while they were still in the school system, which limited their qualification for college enrollment. Limitations emanating from a school system overwhelmingly devoid of male role models, as well as teacher bias reducing their credentials for academic success, are important aspects in explaining why males are now so underrepresented in postsecondary institutions.

Not only should this male underrepresentation in college enrollment and career choices be addressed, but so should the *lack of media acknowledgment* of this problem. Political correctness influences what is brought to the public's attention, and issues related to gender advantage are likely to be avoided if the revelation is that males are the ones who are being subjected to unfair situations. After decades of attention given to female discrimination, the mass media seem hesitant to generate any public debate on male discrimination. Political correctness is today's dominating theme for the media, despite its long-term consequences for our society's economic well-being.

Fortunately, some, albeit limited, media focus on this issue is emerging. One portrayal regarding the pervasive nature of this problem around the world was depicted by Mui (2016) in the *Washington Post*. Figure 8.1, prepared by the OECD, identifies the prime-age male labor-force participation rates across OECD countries, and how these rates have declined between 1990 and 2014.

The emerging concern on this issue is evident across the world; it is acutely evident within the United States and, to a lesser degree, in Canada. Whereas the declining male participation rate in the labor force seems most worrisome in Italy, the American decline is almost as troubling.

Reports on the "missing males" in our workforce contain some conjecture as to the reasons; however, while the lack of educational credentials is identified, seldom are any quantifiable data presented that demonstrate our school systems' contribution to the problem. The complexity of this issue prevents most reporters from attaching any quantification of its impact, but noting how the concern is rooted in our school systems is an important step toward

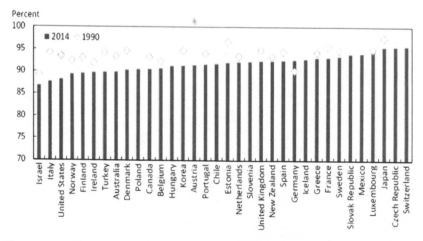

Figure 8.1   Prime-Age Male Labor-Force Participation Rates across the OECD (courtesy of the White House's Council of Economic Advisers)

changing a culture in which quantifiable evidence definitively indicates how male students are being handicapped.

THE KEY POINTS MADE IN THIS CHAPTER ARE:

- A significant percentage of experienced men between the ages of twenty-five and fifty-four withdrew from the labor force between 1990 and 2014.
- Increased globalization and the decline in factory jobs still remaining from the Industrial Age have played a major role in pushing prime-aged men, particularly those with less education, out of the workforce.
- Men in the current generation will soon be enormously underrepresented in the well-paying professions that require a college degree.

Chapter 9

Missing Males

In 1966, James Brown and Betty Jean Newsome released a hit song that characterized the perception of the world at that time, titled "It's a Man's Man's Man's World." A significant cultural change since that time has taken place in many aspects of contemporary society, including within our educational systems. Simply put, males are abandoning the teacher workforce, especially in the younger grades. Males are also gradually being reduced from participating in postsecondary education. Even the workplace, once dominated by males, is now experiencing a lack of males, because so many are simply choosing not to work.

These trends are all impacting our society significantly, but the focus of this chapter is on the most disturbing trend: the *missing males* in our homes. Livingston's (2014) research of the American family brings to our attention some alarming results:

- Fewer than half (46 percent) of American children younger than eighteen years of age are living in a home with two married, heterosexual parents in their first marriage. Seventy-three percent of children fit this description in 1960.
- Thirty-four percent of children today are living in a home with an unmarried parent—up from just 9 percent in 1960.
- A small share of children—4 percent—are living with two cohabiting parents.

The Single Mother website, https://singlemotherguide.com/about/, accessed on September 17, 2016, provides the additional understanding that, in the United States, almost ten million children, or 84 percent of single-parent families, live with a single mother, and 49 percent of those mothers have never married.

The family unit thrived when most of the world lived on a family farm and interdependency was the glue that kept everyone pulling in the same direction. More children provided free labor, especially when the parents grew older and were unable to carry the workload themselves because of declining health or injury. The family unit provided a bonded "team" that struggled through hardships together in a time when few government-support programs existed.

The Industrial Age changed this culture by splitting families apart, as young people began to colonize in large, urban centers, looking for work in factories that were sprouting up across the nation. But still, the family, even though it was somewhat disjointed, had strong bonds, frequently supported by spiritual beliefs, and the family unit remained solid, even though the extended family began to be separated by distance. Children still felt supported by a mother and father who were working together to raise their offspring to become responsible adults.

Today, educators constantly lament the lack of family structure in many households where a school's goals had been actively supported in the home. A call from school personnel used to receive prompt attention, and male adults in the home consistently attended school functions. Modeling from an adult male for young boys was evident in every aspect of life—including the intellectual, social, physical, emotional, and spiritual domains. Much was lost when the "me generation" set aside traditional values, choosing instead to pursue self-gratification, and children became more of an inconvenience to many fathers, who began to "flee the scene."

This brief historical overview is intended to help explain the disadvantage many male students experience in their early school years. Without the benefit of male teachers in primary school, men who understand a male student's specific learning issues and can act as role models in their classrooms, demonstrating positive attitudes and engagement in learning, too many young boys fall behind their female peers.

In our society, placing female teachers in primary school seemed a logical extension of the roles found in a child's early home life, which followed the traditional family situation in which the father worked in a career and the mother worked in the household. Such an environment is now mostly passé, and *it may, even then, not have been in the best interests of young male students*. Educational research has opened up new thinking about how learning differs between the genders and why more male teachers in early grades are necessary for the educational development of young male students.

Injecting substantial numbers of male teachers into the school system's early grades should be a priority in order to overcome the existing negative stereotypes regarding male teachers working with young children. Choosing to work with young children is a gift, because patience is the greatest virtue needed when dealing with such short attention spans in students. However, there is a hurdle to overcome: Male teachers worry that their presence in the primary classroom will be greeted by suspicious parents concerned with having a male working with their young children.

Role models are important to children, and when so many homes are now missing the male role model, *the school system must do more to fulfill its mandate to meet the needs of all students.* Disregard and inaction have made up the modus operandi for too long, and the negative effects of inaction have now become a sad commentary on how schools have failed the nation's males. The fallout is evident in the dramatic gender imbalance now seen in our postsecondary institutions and the subsequent dropout rates of males from the workplace.

The downstream effect on our families is emerging, as the percentages of fatherless homes increase. Experiencing success in school is a significant contributor to all students' self-esteem; however, when this factor is further impacted by the educators' biases outlined in this book, we can only conclude that our schools and their leaders have no regard for fairness. Changing the culture requires at least a two-pronged approach: The first is to strengthen accountability within the school system, and the second is to intervene in staffing programs. Both of these approaches are dealt with in the next and final chapter of this book.

Chapter 10

Righting the Gender Ship

Realistically, how can we respond to this crisis that is so disadvantaging our male students? Some readers may object to efforts for ameliorating this disadvantage by choosing to focus on the sexist theme that has enjoyed phenomenal success in overcoming other societal issues. *The same zeal, passion, and effort are required to correct the unfairness to males in the subject of reading, as has been undertaken on behalf of females in the subjects of mathematics and science.* Avoiding decades more of this unfair situation requires significant and immediate action.

A similar frustration regarding the current indifference about the lack of male success in school surfaced in the United Kingdom's *Guardian* newspaper, written by a member of Parliament (McCartney 2016):

As Lincoln's MP, I have been struck by the underperformance of boys in education compared with girls.... But there is hardly anything being done to tackle it.... Why has there been such little action on the issue? If the genders were reversed, I am almost certain this would not be the case. Indeed for well over 25 years, taxpayers' money has welcomely and successfully been spent on encouraging female applications for science, technology, engineering and mathematics courses in higher education. Yet, there is no or little reciprocal focus on men becoming doctors (two in every three new GPs are female) or lawyers (over three in five trainees are female).

School systems are loath to make this unfairness public, because the public's confidence in their efforts might be diminished. Acknowledging unfairness toward a segment of the student population would be damning evidence that demonstrates how political correctness interferes with common sense, and, in this issue, has created a breach of trust for male students.

A cursory search on the Internet indicates that concern regarding the paucity of male teachers in the early school years is a universal problem, and, worse, nowhere exists a successful, large-scale initiative to change the matter. Imaginations are seemingly fettered by politically correct, sexist thinking that any resolution must be universally applied to both genders. However, out-of-the-box solutions are required, and the nature of teacher preparation requires immediate transformative action so that discrimination against yet another generation of students does not occur.

The current fallout from past discrimination against the female gender has created a need for courage to expose this new trend of discrimination against males. The "sexist trains" are "on the track," and allowing a nonconformist viewpoint to be an interloper presents a logistical hurdle that can be overcome only with a significant media campaign. While some attention in the media has been given to the "missing males" in our society, little information has been reported regarding its causes or the economic fallout.

What is reported is mostly related to choices made by males, such as criminal activity culminating in jail time that deters those involved from being hired in the future, or media reports on career losses associated with society's progression from the Industrial Era to the Information Age. In these examples, affected males are simply expected to adjust and change their career paths, just as females have done. Our competitive environment does not coddle people readily, unless some injustice is obvious.

Such unfairness to young males has been thoroughly documented in this book. *The numbers do not lie.* The period of a person's life is a critical factor here, because children have few defenses to thwart such unfairness. This type of predicament requires government intervention—as government is meant to be the defender of fairness—however, as is too often the case, the prodding of our politicians is necessary. And in our media-driven society, they are the logical vehicle for such prodding.

A broad discussion of the predicament, supported by quantitative research, is the initial need in a campaign to reverse the disturbing trends outlined in this book. Concerns from educators, specifically that public confidence in the school systems will be lost if this information is publicly displayed, must be swept aside. The educational needs of students must be our paramount concern, even though educators present a powerful special-interest group looking to protect their own reputations.

The data story necessary for public disclosure and discussion must be two-pronged, because two inextricably linked issues are in play. The first matter for discussion is well understood, even though it has been mostly kept from public knowledge. Grade inflation reflecting low standards in classrooms has been well researched, with a plethora of studies proving its existence both in North America and Europe. These low standards have given rise to two major

American initiatives: No Child Left Behind, implemented under President George W. Bush, and Race to the Top, initiated under President Barack Obama.

Common Core, while not a federal initiative, was requested by U.S. governors to raise standards across all of the states, but it was ultimately cut down by Congress in 2015, because some politicians believed it too overreaching by the federal government. Other members of Congress were opposed to having the results from the standardized assessments, the *students'* test results, become part of a *teacher's* evaluation and ultimately affect their rate of pay. Common standards pose a threat to those within the school system, including its leadership, because the public finally would possess comparative information regarding how well schools, school districts, and state educational systems were performing.

The second matter, however, is more relevant to the theme of the "missing men" in our workplaces. Grade inflation is disconcerting, because it robs taxpayers from receiving what they are led to believe they are receiving, but it is made more troublesome by our findings that it is not equally applied to all students. Males are most affected by grade inflation because educators are conflating their academic achievement with compliant behavior, thus providing unfair opportunities for more awards, scholarships, and placement in prestigious university programs to female students. Too many males are being robbed of their dreams.

INSTITUTING HIGHER ACCOUNTABILITY

This unfair treatment of male students can be partially or completely resolved; however, establishing a trusting environment, in which everyone is assessed fairly, requires dramatic action. *System-wide assessments utilizing anonymous marking negates biases* currently at play in classrooms where progress is assessed exclusively by the student's classroom teacher. This strategy is contentious, because it communicates directly that *trust has been broken*. Therefore, school systems might adopt a hybrid approach, in which the teacher's assessment counts as only a portion of students' final marks.

Early grades usually follow a progress report that does not assign a specific letter grade or percentage for programs of study but gives an array of symbols—e.g., S for satisfactory. Fairness could still be enhanced, however, by providing a *system-wide assessment* in the core subjects—i.e., language arts, mathematics, science, and social studies—so that teachers can benefit from feedback on their students' success relative to the system standards, *a feature proven to reduce teachers' propensity for grade inflation*. Low standards in classrooms is a problem, but the real culprit is how these low standards are conflated with compliant behaviors—to the detriment of male students.

These system assessments, or standardized tests, can also provide parents with a more accurate perspective on their child's progress relative to grade-level expectations, which could motivate them to pursue learning opportunities for their children beyond those offered by the school. The strength of these assessments is that questions are well researched, using extensive field testing for validity and reliability, and that they cover almost all curriculum outcomes with questions composed to focus on higher-order thinking. Equally important is that at least two teachers should mark these tests anonymously; this is seldom, if ever, the case when teachers assess their own students.

These are critical features for ensuring both accountability and fairness in grading practices, and when any of these are lacking, it calls into question the validity and reliability of classroom assessments. Parents and administrators should be checking whether teachers are employing these features, and school boards should be provided in the public meetings with detailed reports confirming teachers' adherence. The *chain of ambivalence* regarding these important matters *must be broken* so that trust can be earned again.

Progress reporting in the earlier grades is further enhanced when parents are provided with a *summative statement for the two main subject areas—language arts and mathematics*. This statement should utilize *three options* that contribute to a parent's understanding of their child's progress, and it should inform teachers in subsequent grades of the longitudinal summary of each student's progress. Specifically, the summary statement should be: "Academic progress is *'at,' 'above,'* or *'below'* grade level." Some districts codify this process by providing parents with secure access to their child's record on the district's website, where each year's summative statement is recorded.

Accountability and transparency must be the *pillars for reform* in education, as is evidenced by the opposition to these from those within the system. Pressure from this tandem approach should be both the impetus for leadership to examine what is or is not working, and the motivation to achieve improvement throughout their spheres of influence. *People are inclined to measure support rather than pay attention to outcomes, which explains the need for pressure in this area.* The private sector understands the concept of "pressure," but for many in the public sector, using this term connotes a negative situation.

TEACHING TO THE TEST IS A RUSE

Standardized testing has been the most contentious form of pressure within the field of education throughout the previous two decades. Unreasonable statements have been presented by educators *to confuse the public*, so that their voices might dissuade politicians from endorsing policies that also have the potential to place them "under pressure." Ultimately, however, public education is the government's responsibility, and politicians need to be held accountable for the quality of services provided to their constituents.

The most common example of how educators attempt to confuse the public and parents regarding large-scale testing lies in the phrase "teaching to the test." However, "teaching to the test" is an inaccurate and ultimately confusing description. Tests are based on the curriculum—and it would be absurd to test what has not been taught. It is only fair to students that they be taught what is going to be tested. Vociferous and legitimate objections would be voiced by parents if students were tested on content not contained within the curriculum.

Before states and provinces implemented large-scale testing programs, educators used generic tests from testing companies, which were *not curriculum-specific*. These generic tests were developed to accommodate the largest populated regions, such as California in the United States and Ontario in Canada. Yes, most of the test items did fit the curriculum of other regions, but there were always some questions that were not a good match.

While teachers used these generic tests for their own purposes, they objected—rightfully—to any attempt to hold them accountable for the results, because some questions did not relate to their region's curriculum. However, this proved to be a convenient "dodge" for any accountability whatsoever, and it led to today's testing programs in which states and provinces now develop their own tests to match their own curriculum outcomes.

If teachers object to "teaching to the test" that has been prepared for their region, then the question becomes, what are they teaching? If the test has been derived from the lawful curriculum, why is this concept being ridiculed? The reason that so many states underwent the arduous process of building curriculum frameworks in the 1990s was to ensure that all aspects of their curriculum were actually taught. Instructional omissions had been occurring, because teachers were choosing to teach their *preferred curriculum*, sometimes to the exclusion of that mandated by the state. Instead of "teaching *to* the test," should teachers really "teach *away* from the test"?

Phelps (2003) provides a cogent description of this illogical position taken by anti-testing advocates:

> "Teaching to the test" is the perfect "damned if you do, damned if you don't argument." Do not teach the material that will be covered in a test, and you will be excoriated. Teach what will be covered in a test, and you will be excoriated. The only way out, of course, is the solution preferred by testing opponents—[to] stop all testing (and let them run the schools the way they like).

There is significant insight in the final phrase of this description: "Let them run the schools the way they like." This is precisely what has happened with the incursion and intrusion of social promotion into educational practice.

When students are shuffled through our schools without demonstrating sufficient learning or understanding of the curriculum, teachers are forced to adapt
the curriculum to meet their students' academic "needs."

Curriculum adaptation is a good practice for some, *but too many students
are experiencing social promotion because the school system has lost its
accountability of ensuring that students are ready for the next grade.* Too
many teaching practices are employed without a database supporting their
use. Too many effective organizational practices are disregarded and not
implemented.

Tests expose this lack of success. *Tests reveal that there are differences
in teacher quality.* Tests demonstrate that some schools are more effective
than others. Tests provide the indication that some students have been disadvantaged by elements within their educational system. Tests make teachers,
principals, system administrators, and politicians *accountable* for their leadership. They put pressure on these levels of leadership to employ meaningful
improvement strategies. *They are our messengers of excellence and medioc-
rity,* which is the reason some within the system want them "killed." They are
"messengers" that expose shortcomings and make the system feel uncomfortable. Hence the name of Phelps's book, *Kill the Messenger.*

"Teaching *to* the test" is not the real issue. What is objectionable is when
teachers actually "teach the test." Some testing programs use the same tests
for several administrations, and it is possible for some teachers to access the
questions unethically, and then use these actual questions for review in subsequent years before the questions are released for public use. This practice
is *cheating,* because it is *teaching the test*—literally.

What is unacceptable in this slogan, used by unions and educators, mis-
represents aspects of assessment in an attempt to avoid accountability for
providing students with an excellent education. *Educators should actually
be advocating that all aspects of the curriculum be assessed, rather than not
having any assessment at all.* They should be promoting fairness to students
by insisting that gains in student achievement be consistently and persistently
monitored, so that no one—of either gender—falls through the cracks.

Politicians' sympathetic ear to the incoherent arguments of anti-testing
proponents exposes their priorities. Rather than implementing testing
programs that ensure greater fairness to students across the educational
system, they placate educators who are seeking to absent themselves from
accountability for student achievement. By casting their allegiance with
the service providers, they demonstrate an attitude opposed to students'
best interests.

*A critical finding demonstrated in this book is that system-wide testing with
anonymous marking provides a fairer description of learning.* The propensity
for teachers to conflate non-academic issues, such as compliant behavior,
with assessments of student achievement provides a decided advantage to

female students. This unfairness must be arrested, and providing system-wide tests for all grades—3 through 12—will produce amazing consistency in the assessments of student achievement for both genders.

System-wide testing within a region does not resolve entirely the issue raised earlier about marks submitted by postsecondary applicants for institutions across the country. While neither Canada nor the United States has a common set of standards for their country, expectations across the provinces and states are relatively consistent. The logistics of common testing across these two countries, with so many time zones, make synchronistic administrations of national tests difficult, and when this does not happen, the potential for cheating becomes a significant hurdle to overcome.

Therefore, standardized testing within a province or a state can provide a major step for increasing fairness across classrooms, schools, and school districts. Research demonstrates that such a testing program will reduce grade inflation, which then reduces the level of unfairness toward males from classroom assessments influenced by teacher bias. Such an ongoing assessment program can also provide an impetus for improving student achievement—the ultimate goal of the education system.

CAREER MODELING

Staffing schools with more male teachers and role models will be discussed later; however, there are other activities that schools can undertake to bring more adult males into contact with students. Children are motivated to learn when they can link their work in school with the outside world of work. Exposing students to a variety of careers should be an ongoing feature in each school's program—and these efforts should begin in the primary-school grades. Visits to the fire station and the grocery store are examples of experiences frequently utilized in kindergarten, because they are so visible in daily living, because they employ both genders, and because they provide a pace of activity for these learners who have short attention spans.

In subsequent grades, more complex tasks in the workplace should be featured, especially in areas impacted by our new age of technology. Dividing classes into gender groups, who are then assigned to same-gender presenters, is a modeling aspect made critical by our "missing men" era. Our young male students must see and interact with males in the workplace, so that an enthusiasm for work can be transmitted into the students' world.

In the upper grades, brief opportunities for "job shadowing" by young teenagers will provide more in-depth opportunities to learn about skill sets that are necessary in the workplace. In an era when school truancy has become a major concern, reporting to work on time and ready to meet daily work schedules is a primary expectation that students must learn. Maintaining productive relationships, demonstrating an orientation toward service, providing a conscientious effort throughout the workday, and being able to learn elementary specifics in a career of interest are valuable skills that will help students achieve success in their current "workplace" of school, as well as orient them toward a successful career later in life.

Naturally, these experiences are beneficial for all students; however, our current societal crisis requires a special focus on our male students. The lack of a workable budget is frequently used as an excuse for a lack of action in this area, and so priorities must be determined that target specific needy populations. Targeted budgets have always been used in education, and they were certainly implemented when females required greater exposure to STEM courses. Focusing on resolving our concerns regarding male students should be as self-explanatory as special funding allocations for female students were in the past.

Another example of career modeling, with a special focus on teaching, is that of a "buddy system." Again, personal experience has demonstrated how educationally worthwhile this activity is for all students. The buddy system can focus on reading and math, but for males, it might be better focused primarily on reading, which is the curricular area that research demonstrates as the greatest need.

Implementation of this strategy is not difficult. In an elementary school, older students are assigned to be a special "buddy" to learners in grades 1 and 2. The older students, during specific times arranged by the staff, meet with their younger buddies to read and interact with them, so that the early learners can practice their reading skills without worrying what their classroom peers might think about them. The younger students already expect their older listeners to be more accomplished, and therefore self-esteem issues are less threatening because direct comparisons are avoided. A spinoff of this partnership is also evident on the playground, where the relationship between "buddies" can deepen.

Experience has also demonstrated the benefits of similar endeavors implemented between older elementary school students who are "buddied" with nearby middle-school students. Travel time is an obvious limitation; however, where this is not a factor, and where middle-school students have option programs in place, such partnerships can evolve for the benefit of both older and younger students. Not only is the younger student able to practice identified academic skills, but the older student is placed in a position to experience the positive aspects of working with younger children. The seed of a possible career in education is sown.

Researchers have found that superior teacher talent is related to early interest in a career in teaching. When "outstanding" teachers were interviewed, many indicated that their initial interest in teaching had occurred by the end of grade 6. These buddy events sponsored within schools can provide opportunities for young students to experience the emotional "highs" that come from helping primary-aged students be more successful.

It should be understood that schools cannot be expected to do everything; the community also has an obligation to contribute toward developing positive attitudes toward work within the next generation. Whether these arrangements are formalized, through a community program or simply by concerned citizens assuming leadership roles, all adults can provide work-related experiences for the young citizens of their community. This initiative is also a "buddy system" between generations, in which the outcome, again, is more than merely focusing on work preparation.

One personal example occurred when a neighbor observed the author as a young boy, hitting rocks across a roadway into an empty field. Concerned that the young hitter might not be sufficiently mature to discern when conditions were safe for such an activity, the older neighbor introduced himself and suggested a trip to the local golf course. After outfitting this young boy with a set of clubs and an annual golf membership, which would be reimbursed by the younger neighbor cutting his lawn and doing other odd jobs, this older mentor arranged with five friends to have their lawns also cut—an arrangement that lasted for six years.

This gift from one generation to the next did not end upon the younger neighbor's graduation from high school. Once settled into a career after his university education, a ten-year period followed in which this citizen met several times a weekend with a hundred young people from a church youth group, which, because these events were restricted to high-school students, actually totaled several hundred youth. These times were all voluntary—and seldom was a weekend missed during the span of those ten years. A gratifying outcome of this "giving back" was to see how many of these high schoolers later, during their adulthood, fulfilled similar roles for the generation following them.

Another illustration involves a criminal lawyer who also desired to invest in the next generation and did so for decades but on a smaller scale. His involvement with the criminal justice system made him aware of which young people were living too close to a dangerous edge. Every weekend he employed some of these young boys to perform odd jobs on his acreage. When this community-minded lawyer passed away suddenly, his funeral was a community event. His service to others was appropriately celebrated.

These examples provide suggestions for methods that a community, including its schools, might consider to provide their youth, especially their males, with role models in the workplace. *We must do more than just worry* about the lack of males in the workplace today, and instead plan early interventions to prepare our youth for success later in their lives.

MALE ROLE MODELS IN THE CLASSROOM

Providing male role models in the classroom is the most important need right now in our school systems, with *the exception of using standardized testing accompanied by anonymous marking.* Standardized tests are contentious, because they put a sharper focus on accountability, which too many educators shun, while the modeling aspect addresses the gender issue. This crosses the line of political correctness, and increasing the percentage of male educators in our classrooms requires confronting several myths.

First, and perhaps foremost, educating young students has been labeled incorrectly as "women's work." When I was a student teacher and assigned a lesson of teaching young students, the parade of university supervisors into my classroom was intimidating. Their main focus was to observe how this young, aspiring male teacher would "survive" working with students characterized by short attention spans. Fortunately, my lesson was a success, and similar assignments as a regular teacher followed. Later, as a school administrator, I identified and placed several male teachers in early childhood education who provided stellar service.

However, unfounded suspicions evident in our modern culture regarding males working with young children is worrisome, and it will require government intervention to interrupt the current unfairness experienced by young male students. The lack of male role models willing to step up is also worrisome. The metaphor about turning around a speedboat or an oil tanker comes to mind, because we do not have a long period of time to achieve necessary change. Therefore, two strategies for quickly achieving gender balance in our elementary schools are provided below.

FINANCIAL INCENTIVES

The capacity for money to motivate action cannot be discounted. Our university's faculties of education can use this basic strategy to generate interest in young male high school graduates toward a career in elementary school teaching. Providing scholarships to attract males into elementary school teaching programs is one means to promote interest in pursuing this rewarding career. Scholarships also communicate the importance of having male teachers working with younger students, and that overcoming the current stigma in our culture is a worthy objective.

The second initiative for attracting male teachers into elementary schools is more complex, but it has a considerably greater potential for achieving the objective. The North American marketplace is based on free-market principles, wherein citizens choose their own careers, and remuneration for services provided is undoubtedly a factor in a person's final career choice. A career in teaching is usually not considered a financially rewarding one, because young people are relatively naïve regarding financial issues and they usually focus on salary benefits alone.

To illustrate this naïveté, a conversation with a university president regarding hiring professors revealed an astonishing fact. In the president's opinion, professors almost always made their selection regarding where to teach solely on the basis of salary, even when the cost-of-living factor demonstrated a better financial situation with a different choice. His words—"Professors did not have the financial smarts to realize the difference"—underscores the reason that many young people, especially males, disregard a career in teaching today.

A usual thought process for workers entering the workforce is to examine the starting salaries and evaluate how much those salaries will increase over time. *Benefit costs are seldom considered in their calculations,* and there are a myriad of additional benefits wrapped into a typical teacher salary package. Pensions, paid sick leave, discretionary days, preparation time, as well as many other types of releases from work, both paid and unpaid, can cost taxpayers approximately *25 percent* of a teacher's annual salary.

Life after work is made considerably easier by having a pension, which is partially funded by the taxpayer, but it operates as a consistently applied savings program. Too many citizens employ a happenstance method of saving for retirement, which can be conveniently interrupted for vacation junkets or material desires. The stability of an educator's pension plan is most appreciated after retirement, especially when inflation clauses are included. Therefore, if a teacher's annual salary is $80,000, and the benefits of approximately 25 percent are then factored in, the cost, or the value, to that teacher, becomes $100,000.

There remains one additional factor seldom discussed or even considered by job-hunting graduates. The teachers' vacation package is the most generous of any other career. Having approximately *thirteen weeks of vacation per year* is a sensitive issue among educators, because they typically object to having the additional ten weeks of vacation time—scheduled during summer's prime-time vacation season—beyond most careers actually factored into their compensation. Yet this benefit is almost always conveniently "forgotten" during negotiations, when teacher representatives compare salaries with other employee groups that receive only three or less weeks of annual vacation time.

This form of doublespeak at the bargaining table must be exposed, because this additional vacation time equates to approximately a 15 percent perk—which is a significant financial incentive. Any discussion of salary that ignores this cost factor is meaningless. Therefore, career-minded high-school graduates should consider a teaching career with a teacher's salary of $80,000, plus a benefit package worth $20,000 and an extended vacation package worth 15 percent or $12,000—for a total of $112,000.

Many teachers, however, view the *extended vacation time as a detriment*, because they would prefer the money rather than the time off of work. In this present arrangement, these teachers then enter another part of the workforce in the summer months to supplement their income. Some teachers see an additional job as a necessity to support their families, while others view it as an opportunity to achieve a higher lifestyle. For this latter group, such an opportunity is perceived as a bonus.

These details are provided because they provide a potential solution to several issues within the education system. Recall that the objective is to increase the number of male teachers in the elementary schools, and *this situation is so dire that immediate success is required.* Money is the only leverage capable of achieving swift results without the government actually directing people into careers—an unacceptable alternative in our modern and free society.

Offering male high school graduates a career as an elementary school teacher with an additional 15 percent salary and *their corresponding commitment to undertake a normal work year with only three weeks of paid vacation* provides a reasonable incentive. This concept avoids any conflict with the politically charged, gender-related rhetoric of *equal work, equal pay.* Any suggestion to pay one gender more is unacceptable, especially since there was a time in education when males were the ones who were paid more.

Increasing the work year is a defensible proposition, however, and these twelve-month employees of the school system could undertake multiple tasks during the traditional summer vacation time. Research demonstrates that children from disadvantaged homes learn at the same pace as their more advantaged peers during a normal school year, but their rate of forgetting the material they had learned during the summer vacation is greater, because they do not have similar opportunities for travel, camps, or access to the library (Dueck 2014).

Therefore, many school districts now adopt compensatory summer programs for students, so that learning is more continuous. Rather than experiencing the "forgetting time," many students can maintain a learning pace similar to what might occur during the shorter Christmas break. Full-year teachers can fulfill these summer break assignments, as well as other tasks related to curriculum development and assessment of learning.

This concept of employing male elementary school teachers for a full year could be expanded to include other interested teachers. School districts might wish to serve their communities during the long summer vacation by providing an array of programs, such as remediation, enrichment, technology, sports, arts, etc. All or some of these programs could be provided by teachers already in the school system who want to work for a full term and earn the additional salary. Naturally, funding would be the significant issue that must be addressed, and *this author is committed to recommend strategies that are cost-neutral—i.e., funds that can be found within existing budgets.*

FUNDING FOR FULL-YEAR TEACHERS

Summer programs might be considered a community option, and programs outside of the initiative to incorporate more male teachers in elementary schools can operate with an enrollment fee. This source of funding may be insufficient, however, and identifying more permanent funding could require some reallocation. During a TED Talk with Andreas Schleicher, who manages the PISA international testing program (Dueck 2015), he stated:

> One way you can spend money is by paying teachers well, and you can see Korea investing a lot in attracting the best people into the teaching profession. And Korea also invests into long school days, which drives up costs further. Last but not least, Koreans want their teachers not only to teach but also to develop. They invest in professional development and collaboration and many other things. All that costs money. How can Korea afford all of this? The answer is, students in Korea learn in large classes…. You go to the next country on the list, Luxembourg, and you can see the red dot (representing cost per student) is exactly where it is for Korea, so Luxembourg spends the same per student as Korea does. But, you know, parents and teachers and policymakers in Luxembourg all like small classes. You know, it's very pleasant to walk into a small class. So they have invested all their money into there…. Class size is driving costs up. But even Luxembourg can spend its money only once, and the *price* for this is that teachers are not paid particularly well. Students don't have long hours of learning. And basically, teachers have little time to do anything else than teaching. So you can see two countries spent their money very differently, and actually how they spent their money matters a lot more than how much they invest in education.

North American school systems allocate a high percentage of their funding on class size reduction; however, results on improving student achievement are questionable. Barber and Mourshed reviewed research from around the world and reported their findings in their 2007 McKinsey Report:

> The available evidence suggests that except at the very early grades, class size reduction does not have much impact on student outcomes. Of 112 studies, which looked at the impact of the reduction in class sizes on student outcomes, only 9 found any positive relationship, 103 found either no significant

relationship, or a significant negative relationship. Even when a significant relationship was found the effect was not substantial.

Most importantly, every single one of the studies showed that within the range of class sizes typical in OECD countries, variations in teacher quality completely dominate any effect of reduced class size. At best, reducing class sizes from 23 to 15 students improves achievement by an average student by 8 %ile points.

These authors point out that having more teachers in the school system *requires more hiring from the bottom of the talent pool* (Dueck 2014). There is merit to their claim that class size reduction is counterproductive, because *the quality of the education system cannot exceed the quality of its teachers.*

Governments intent on restoring fairness to males in our school system may reconsider the merit of placing such a *high priority on reducing teacher workload* at the expense of *students' learning conditions.* Increasing male participation in elementary schools involves a relatively minor expense when compared with the significant sums allocated to ongoing initiatives for reducing class sizes.

In another strategy for releasing funds sufficient to pay for increasing elementary school, male teacher participation is articulated in a student registration proposal (Dueck 2013). The current design of a *single entry during a twelve-month window* disadvantages students born in the second half of the year. Implementing a *dual-entry* strategy, with six-year-old students entering the school system every six months, would reduce student failure by 60 percent, increase student achievement by a minimum of 5 percent, and provide the education system with a financial savings of up to 10 percent. In other words, it would achieve *higher levels of student achievement at considerably less cost.*

These are two significant areas from which the education system could reallocate funds without having a negative impact on student learning. Education is a substantial portion of governments' budgets, and, unfortunately, it has many areas in which taxpayers are not receiving "bang for the buck." For example, many studies conclude that most teachers who acquire a master's degree in education do not produce any higher levels of student achievement. Dueck (2014) provides a succinct summary from the U.S. secretary of education:

In November (2010), U.S. Education Secretary Arne Duncan singled out the $8 billion spent on master's degree bonuses annually as wasteful, claiming there is "little evidence [that] teachers with master's degrees improve students' achievement more than other teachers—with the possible exception of teachers who earn master's [degrees] in math and science," according to a speech he gave to the American Enterprise Institute.

These examples are merely a few possible means for deriving the necessary funding to support transformative approaches for reforming education. Unfairness to students, such as is evident with males, requires dramatic and immediate action because "Band-Aid solutions" will not resolve the problem. This book acknowledges past and present discriminations against females, but its primary purpose is to demonstrate how males are currently experiencing serious disadvantages within the education system. The trail outlining these disadvantages—experienced by too many males—progresses as follows:

- Seldom are primary-age males taught by male teachers, who can better understand how young boys learn and behave. Therefore, boys fall behind right away in critical reading skills, and their progress in learning is downgraded when teachers conflate their student achievement with their less compliant behavior.
- Conflating student achievement with behavior remains an ongoing issue throughout males' schooling, and it disqualifies many male students from participating in high-school programs necessary for entry to universities.
- Grade inflation is a significant educational problem, made more serious by its unequal application across the two genders. Therefore, female students benefit more from inflated classroom assessments and they win more awards, scholarships, and placements in universities.
- Standardized testing neutralizes grade inflation, because students' work is assessed anonymously.
- Without a role for exit examinations in decisions regarding university applications, many male students are unable to pursue their career dreams.
- Disenchanted by their options, too many males then become "missing" from today's workforce—and family life—posing a threat to the nation's economic and societal well-being.

THE KEY POINTS MADE IN THIS CHAPTER ARE:

- Out-of-the-box solutions for the lack of male teachers in primary-school grades are required, and the nature of teacher preparation requires immediate transformative action so that another generation of students is not discriminated against.
- Grade inflation is a significant problem, held in check by standardized testing.
- Educators' use of the phrase "teaching to the test" is a ruse.
- Many strategies exist to create opportunities for young male students to interact with male role models in the community.

- Comparing teacher salaries with other professions is inappropriate when benefits, including lengthy vacations, are not factored into the comparison.
- "Equal work, equal pay" is a slogan that cannot be trivialized. Therefore, financial incentives meant to increase the percentage of males in elementary classrooms should focus on expanding the existing work year and eliminating the lengthy summer vacation.
- A program to offer teachers an expanded work year can be readily funded by reallocating existing and wasteful spending.

References

"A-Level Results: Grade Inflation Is Just a Cruel Confidence Trick." *The Telegraph*, August 20, 2009.

Babcock, P. "Real Costs of Nominal Grade Inflation? New Evidence from Student Course Evaluations." *Economic Inquiry* 48, no. 4, October 2010.

Barber, M., and Mourshed, M. *How the World's Best-Performing School Systems Come Out on Top*. New York: McKinsey, 2007.

Bevan, Y., Brighouse, T., Mills, G., Rose, J., and Smith, M. *Report of the Expert Group on Assessment*. 2009. http://publications.education.gov.uk/eOrderingDownload/Expert-Group-Report.pdf.

Bronson, L. *Single-Gender Education: Does It Work?* River Forest, IL: Dominican University, 2012.

Bushway, A., and Nash, W. R. "School Cheating Behaviour." *Review of Educational Research* 47, no. 4, 1977.

Cassidy, S. "Gender Gap in Teaching Grows: Only 24% of New Recruits Are Men." *Independent*, September 25, 2008.

Craft, H. "The Myth of Teacher Objectivity in Student Assessment." *Controversial Issues in Public Education* (blog), September 24, 2014. http://teachingdoneright.blogspot.com/search?q=business+of+determining+student+grades.

Davis, S. F., Drinan, P. F., and Gallant, T. B. *Cheating in School*. West Sussex, UK: Wiley-Blackwell, 2009.

Decoo, W. *Crisis on Campus: Confronting Academic Misconduct*. Cambridge, MA: MIT Press, 2002.

Drolet, D. "Minding the Gender Gap." *AU University Affairs*, September 10, 2007.

Dueck, J. *Being Fair with Kids*. Lanham, MD: Rowman & Littlefield, 2013.

Dueck, J. *Education's Flashpoints*. Lanham, MD: Rowman & Littlefield, 2014.

Dueck, J. *How Political Correctness Weakens Schools*. Lanham, MD: Rowman & Littlefield, 2015.

Feller, B. "Teacher's Gender Affects Learning." Associated Press, August 27, 2006.

French, J. "Are Teachers Inflating Grades?" *Edmonton Journal*, February 27, 2017.

Frenette, M., and Zeman, K. "Why Are Most University Students Women? Evidence Based on Academic Performance, Study Habits and Parental Influences" (research paper). Statistics Canada, September 2007.

Harlen, W. "A systematic review of the evidence of the impact on students, teachers and the curriculum of the process of using assessment by teachers for summative purposes." In *Research Evidence in Education Library.* London: EPPI-Centre, Social Science Research Unit, Institute of Education, 2004.

Hoffmann, F., and Oreopoulos, P. "A Professor Like Me: The Influence of Instructor Gender on College Achievement." *Journal of Human Resources* 44, no. 2, 2009.

Johnson, T. "Are Boys or Girls Better at School?" *Canadian Family,* April 2009.

Jost, K. "Grade Inflation." *CQ Researcher,* June 7, 2002.

Karas, K. "Reason for gender gap in universities debated." *The Globe and Mail,* January 6, 2011.

King, K., and Gurian, M. "With Boys in Mind/Teaching to the Minds of Boys." *Educational Leadership* 64, no. 1, September 2006.

Koedel, C. "Grade inflation for education majors and low standards for teachers." *American Enterprise Institute,* No. 7, August 2011.

Laurie, L. *Grade inflation sets up students to fail: Study.* Halifax, Nova Scotia: Atlantic Institute for Marketing, 2007.

Lawson, H. "Girls get higher marks at school than boys because they are better behaved." *Daily Mail Online,* April 1, 2013.

"Learning and Gender." *American School Board Journal* (October 2006).

Lessons in Learning: Why Boys Don't Like to Read: Gender Differences in Reading Achievement. Canadian Council on Learning (February 2009).

Livingston, G. "Fewer than half of U.S. kids today live in a 'traditional' family." Pew Research Center, December 22, 2014. http://www.pewresearch.org.

Lopez, M., and Gonzalez-Barrera, A. "Women's college enrollment gains leave men behind." Pew Research Center, March 6, 2014. http://www.pewresearch.org.

Martin, S. "Gender gap widens as women graduates outpace the men." *The Australian,* August 15, 2015.

McCabe, D., Trevino, L., and Butterfield, K. "Cheating in Academic Institutions: A Decade of Research." *Ethics and Behavior* 11, part 3, 2001.

McCartney, K. "Our schools are failing boys, which is bad news for Britain." *The Guardian,* September 6, 2016.

McClure, M. "National Standards Sought for Exams." *Calgary Herald,* November 29, 2011.

Mui, Y. "Why America's Men Aren't Working." *Washington Post,* June 20, 2016.

National Post Editorial Board. "Fight the Stigma Against Male Teachers." *National Post,* February 20, 2013.

Newberger, E. *The Men They Will Become: The Nature and Nurture of the Male Character.* Reading, MA: Perseus Publishing, 1999.

Niels, G. *Top Reasons Why Students Cheat.* About.com, January 17, 2014.

OECD. "Grade Expectations: How Marks and Education Policies Shape Students' Ambitions." *PISA,* OECD Publishing, 2012. http://dx.doi.org/10.1787/97892641 87528-en.

Phelps, R. *Kill the Messenger: The War on Standardized Testing.* New Brunswick, NJ: Transaction Publishers, 2003.

Phelps, R. "The Role and Importance of Standardized Testing in the World of Teaching and Training." A paper presented at the 15th Congress of the World for Educational Research, June 3, 2008.

Porter, L. "The Great Man Shortage Hits Australian Classrooms." *Sydney Morning Herald*, November 8, 2015.

Pratt, S. "What about those diploma exams?" *Edmonton Journal*, November 28, 2011.

"Pupils Make More Effort with Male Teachers as They Are Seen as 'More Fair.'" *Daily Mail*, November 13, 2010.

Ratcliffe, R. "The gender gap at universities: where are all the men?" *The Guardian*, January 29, 2013.

Rocheleau, M. "On campus, women outnumber men more than ever." *Boston Globe*, March 28, 2016.

Ryan, J. "Student Plagiarism in an Online World." *ASEE Prism Magazine*, December 1998.

Sands, A. "Would Shakespeare Earn an A?" *Edmonton Journal*, May 24, 2014.

Scantlebury, K. "Gender Bias in Teaching." Education.com, December 23, 2009.

Steffenhagen, J. "UBC Acknowledges Tougher Grading in Alberta." *Vancouver Sun*, March 22, 2012.

Thomas, M. D., and Bainbridge, W. "Grade Inflation: The Current Fraud." *Effective School Research*, January 1997.

Turcotte, M. "Women and Education." *Women in Canada: A Gender-based Statistical Report* (Statistics Canada) (December 2011).

Voyer, D. "Girls Make Higher Grades Than Boys in All School Subjects, Analysis Finds." American Psychological Association, April 29, 2014. http://www.apa.org.

Wall, C. *The Skewing of the Bell Curve: A Study of Grade Inflation in Oklahoma High Schools.* University of Oklahoma, 2003. http://biosurvey.ou.edu/oas/03/paper/wall.htm (site discontinued).

Webber, C., Aitken, N., Lupart, J., and Scott, S. *The Alberta Student Assessment Study.* Edmonton: The Crown in Right of Alberta, 2009.

Woods, M. "Making the Grade." *Queen's Journal*, September 19, 2008.